Scotland

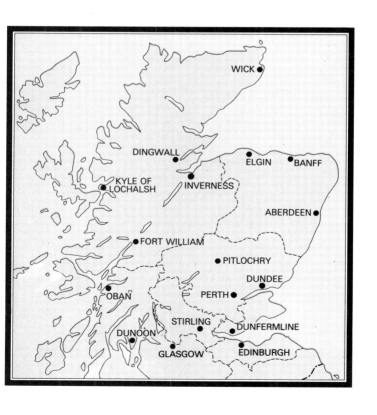

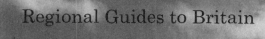

Regional Guides to Britain

Scotland

Frank Thompson
Series Editor **Kenneth Lowther**

Ward Lock Limited · London

© Ward Lock Limited 1983
First published in Great Britain in 1983
by Ward Lock Limited, 82 Gower Street,
London WC1E 6EQ, a Pentos Company.

Designed by Peter Holroyd
Maps by Clyde Surveys Ltd, Maidenhead

Text filmset in Century Schoolbook
by MS Filmsetting Limited, Frome, Somerset

Printed in Great Britain by
M & A Thomson Litho Ltd., East Kilbride, Scotland

British Library Cataloguing in Publication Data
Thompson, Frank
    Scotland.—(Regional guides to Britain)
    1. Scotland—Description and travel—Guide-books
    I. Title   II. Series
    914.11'04858   DA867

ISBN 0-7063-6218-7 Pbk

The black and white photographs were kindly supplied
by the following:
p. 2/3, A. F. Kersting; p. 23, Gavin B. McIntosh;
p. 153, Scottish Tourist Board; p. 73, Bob Swan.
All other photographs by British Tourist Authority.

Frontispiece: Glencoe

Contents

Aberdeen 53

Aberdeen – Cults – Peterculter – Crathes – Banchory –
Aboyne – Balmoral – Ballater – Braemar –
Cairnwell/Glen Shee – Strathdon – Kildrummy – Alford –
Craigievar – Midmar – Echt – Aberdeen

Banff 63

Banff – Macduff – Gardenstown – Pennan – New Aberdour –
Rosehearty – Fraserburgh – Rathen – Peterhead – Boddam –
Port Errol – Ellon – Pitmedden – Oldmeldrum – Huntly –
Rothiemay – Fordyce – Portsoy – Whitehills – Banff

Elgin 74

Elgin – Fochabers – Keith – Craigellachie – Dufftown –
Tomintoul – Grantown-on-Spey – (Aviemore) – Ardclach –
Nairn – Auldearn – Elgin

Inverness 84

Inverness – Beauly – Kilmorack – Struy – Cannich –
Drumnadrochit – Invermoriston – Fort Augustus – Foyers –
Dores – Inverness

Dingwall 93

Dingwall – Strathpeffer – Contin – Garve – Ullapool –
Ledmore – (Lochinver) – Invercassley – Invershin –
Bonar Bridge – Alness – Evanton – Dingwall

Wick 100

Wick – Keiss – Freswick – John o' Groats – Mey –
Castletown – Thurso – Scrabster – Dounreay – Melvich –
Bettyhill – Strathnaver – Strath of Kildonan – Helmsdale –
Dunbeath – Latheron – Wick

Kyle of Lochalsh 109

Tour of Wester Ross
Kyle of Lochalsh – Balmacara – Eilean Donan – Stromeferry –
Strathcarron – Achnasheen – Kinlochewe – Inverewe –
Torridon – Shieldaig – Kishorn – Lochcarron – Plockton –
Kyle of Lochalsh

Eilean Donan Castle

Introduction

The area covered in this regional guide book covers more than one quarter of the land mass of Britain and over one half of Scotland. A first reaction might be to wonder how the visitor to Scotland could even begin to get the flavour of a country which manages to cram an astonishing variety of scenery into its small area, from high stark mountains, bleak moorland and rolling fields to tortuous sea lochs and more than a scattering of islands. Yet, it is possible to obtain more than a superficial insight into a country which, despite its size, has made a mark on the world out of proportion to its population and its area. Its history book has pages seething with instances of intellectual vigour, religious dissension, scientific innovation, technical discovery and cultural achievement. And often this has been through Scotland's languages of English, Scots (sometimes called Lallans) and Gaelic. Almost every corner has produced folk who have had a say in the making of Scotland's history, her landscape and her culture.

This book, then, offers the visitor the chance to become acquainted with the diversity which is Scotland, in a number of suggested tours, each of which offers a full day's intake of things to see, things to do and, on occasion, food to sample for the cuisine of Scotland at its best is a delight. The fact that this book, for reasons of limited space, covers Scotland only north of Glasgow and Edinburgh, should not deter the visitor from spending some time in the south, in the Borders area, where broad sweeping hills gladden the eye and where so much of Scotland's turbulent past history is still to be seen in ruined keeps and castles.

Thanks to an excellent network of tourist and visitor centres throughout the country, there is always on hand the local expertise and knowledge which will make each tour route something to remember, which will long linger in the memory and perhaps entice the visitor to Scotland back again for a second helping.

This book could not have been written without the help of those who are professionally involved in making the visitor to Scotland more than welcome. The quality of their assistance has impressed me, as it will those who decide to put Scotland on their itinerary. If they get as much pleasure as the writer has had in compiling this book, then the purpose of this guide will have been achieved.

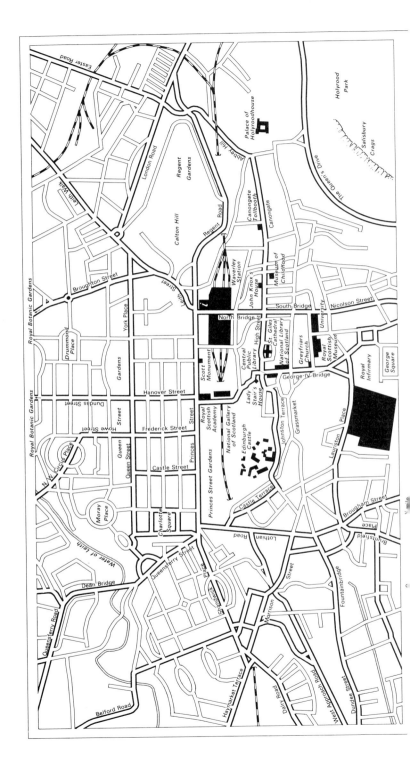

Edinburgh

Tourist Information Centre
5 Waverley Bridge, tel 226 6591

Population 449,907

Theatres
King's Theatre, Leven Street, Tollcross
Royal Lyceum, Grindlay Street
Playhouse, Greenside Place
Traverse, West Bow
Adam House, Chambers Street

Cinemas
Classic, Nicolson Street
ABC, Lothian Road
Odeon, Clerk Street
Caley, Lothian Road
Cameo, Home Street
Edinburgh Film Theatre, Randolph Crescent

Concert Hall
Usher Hall, Lothian Road

Places of Interest
Edinburgh Castle. The castle stands on a rise of ground which presents
Princes Street with its world-famous backcloth. The site of the castle
has been a fortification from the earliest times, certainly before the
sixth century. The pages of its history are full of violence, intrigue and
important historic events such as the birth, in 1566, of James VI, whose
mother was Mary, Queen of Scots. James was later to become James I
of England. During the Napoleonic Wars French prisoners were held
here. Within the castle are many displays of its past. The Crown Room
holds the Scottish Regalia (Crown, Sceptre and Sword of State); the
crown dates from King Robert the Bruce, is made from Scottish gold
and was last used at the coronation of Charles II at Scone in 1651.
Queen Mary's Apartments contain many relics of the Jacobite Risings.
Other features of interest include the Scottish National War
Memorial, the old Parliament Hall, St Margaret's Chapel (built by
Queen Margaret in 1076) and the Scottish United Services Museum,
which has displays covering the history and uniforms of all three
armed services.

Holyroodhouse. The buildings here include the Palace and the ruined
Abbey. The latter was founded in 1128 and was to be the scene of many
events in Scottish history. It fell into ruins in 1768 when the roof
collapsed after the building had been reconstructed with stonework
too heavy for the structure to support. The Palace is kept in a fine
state of preservation and is the official residence of Her Majesty the
Queen when she is in Edinburgh. There are many rooms with fine

paintings, tapestries and furniture. Of particular interest is the Picture Gallery where the portraits of 111 Scottish kings look down on visitors. Some of the portraits were derived from the painter's (Jacob de Wet) fertile imagination.

St Giles' Cathedral, High Street. The present building dates from the fifteenth century, though the site has been occupied since the ninth century. Much of the exterior of the church has been restored. The real, almost tangible, atmosphere belongs to the interior of the building where there are many monuments to famous Scots; the colours of Scottish Regiments hang in the nave. The Chapel of the Thistle belongs to Scotland's premier order, consisting of the monarch and sixteen knights.

Museum of Childhood, High Street. This is a marvellously comprehensive display, more intended, one suspects, for adults than children. Here one can go back in time and re-live what children once read, ate, played and collected.

John Knox's House, High Street. This building, dating in part from the fifteenth century, contains most attractive wood panelling and displays material from the period of John Knox, the sixteenth-century religious reformer.

Lady Stair's House, Lawnmarket. This seventeenth-century house is a museum containing mementoes of Robert Burns, Sir Walter Scott and Robert Louis Stevenson.

Canongate Tolbooth. This is a sixteenth-century town hall which is now a museum with displays including the Highland dress.

The Scott Monument, Princes Street. This is an ornate Victorian memorial to Sir Walter Scott. If you have enough breath, 287 steps invite you to climb them to get to the top. The view along Princes Street and to the Castle is worth the effort.

Georgian House, No. 7 Charlotte Square. This is a restored house of the nineteenth century in the care of the National Trust for Scotland. Everything in the house exudes the way of life of the Georgian wealthy Edinburgh citizen. The kitchen is a marvel to see.

Royal Botanic Gardens, Inverleith Row. The Gardens contain many rare and exotic plants. It is not so well known that many gardens in the British Isles owe part of their beauty to plants originally brought back to Britain in the nineteenth century by Scots explorers and botanists from all corners of the world. Inverleith Gardens will enchant, enthrall and entertain even those who may not particularly care for gardening but love plants.

Edinburgh Zoo, Corstorphine. There is a good collection of animals and birds and reptiles, with many side attractions to complete an enjoyable, if expensive, day's outing.

Royal Scottish Academy, Princes Street. The building was founded in 1826 and exists to display the creations of artists in Scotland. There are usually two main exhibitions each year (summer and during the Edinburgh Festival).

National Gallery of Scotland, The Mound. The gallery contains collections of Scottish artists and has a comprehensive display of sculpture and paintings of European artists, from the sixteenth century to the present, including Degas, Tintoretto, Corot, Claude, Vermeer, Gainsborough, Turner, Monet, van Gogh, Renoir, Goya, Rubens and Titian.

Princes Street Gardens. One of the city's lungs. The Gardens are divided into East and West by The Mound (the steep hill running from the Old Town down to Princes Street). There are many statues of famous Scots. See the American War Memorial, erected by Americans of Scots blood and calling. The Floral Clock is supposed to be the oldest of its kind in the world. Two churches at the west end are worth seeing: St John's (largely nineteenth century) and St Cuthbert's (built on a seventh-century religious site).

National Library of Scotland, George IV Bridge. It contains a bewildering collection of books and documents and rare manuscripts. Exhibitions are frequent on themes of Scottish literary interest. Opposite the National Library is the Central Public Library, which has Scottish and Edinburgh Rooms.

Royal Scottish Museum, Chambers Street. Established in 1854, it has a comprehensive collection of objects ranging from dinosaurs to space suits. Thematic displays are often arranged.

Greyfriars Church, George IV Bridge. Famous for its statue of Greyfriars Bobby, a Skye terrier, which refused to be moved from its master's grave for a period of fourteen years. Greyfriars Churchyard, on the site of a fifteenth-century Franciscan friary, contains many curious tombs. It is the place where the National Covenant of Scotland was signed in 1638.

With some justification Edinburgh can lay claim to being one of the most beautiful cities in Europe. Of course it has, like any other city, its unattractive parts – such as long streets where monotonous and repetitive lines of houses weary the eye, and where only the presence of trees hides the fact that cities must also house many people in the cheapest way possible. But these areas apart, Edinburgh does offer the visitor such a variety of attractions that many return visits are necessary to come really to know this 'Athens of the North'. It is a city where time seems to warp unexpectedly. One moment a walk down a street lined with graceful buildings becomes a journey into the eighteenth-century past, where the Scotland of old comes to life and where the noise of past historical events takes on a reality which stays with one for a long time afterwards. The next moment one is confronted with vistas which simply charm the dullest mind. There are also areas in Edinburgh which display a feeling of wilderness, so much so that one might not accept one was in a city at all. Edinburgh has streets which have changed little since great men, who made their mark in many fields of human endeavour, walked them going about their professional business. Any visitor worth his salt will find it hard to resist the temptation to drop names when describing Edinburgh to friends. Here Robert Louis Stevenson lived. Here Sir Walter Scott wrote. There Robert Burns entertained the gentility of Edinburgh with his poetry. Here lived Deacon Brodie, the factual model for the fictional character of Dr Jekyll and Mr Hyde. There was the house where Alexander Graham Bell was born, the inventor of the telephone. And so it goes on: an almost endless list of names.

Another of Edinburgh's attractions is the fact that it is, like Rome, a city built on hills. There is no need for skyscrapers to hide vast areas of flat land. Rather the undulating land on which Edinburgh is built presents many vistas with a human dimension that is easily appreciated. The 'New Town' part of the city was planned in the eighteenth century by men with vision who decided that beauty was an integral part of architectural creation. And what they managed to achieve is, thankfully, to be seen today in elegant streets, Georgian buildings with character, and tree-lined squares and gardens. Visit Drummond Place to get the feel of being transported back more than a century, particularly in early evening where only the modern dress of a passer-by provides a link with the present. There is a wonderful sense of unity of design in, say, Charlotte Square at the west end of George Street; at the other end, St Andrews Square presents a grander scene.

The 'Old Town' still lives, however. Over the years, restoration has taken place in keeping with the atmosphere of the sixteenth and seventeenth centuries and, despite the roar of noisy traffic on High Street, a strong impression is conveyed of the life lived by the lively people who once populated the old town. The Royal Mile, running down from Edinburgh Castle to the Palace of Holyrood, is full of surprises. Many narrow alleyways, 'closes' and wynds lead into small courtyards, above which tower restored tenement buildings, some with turret staircases spiralling up one corner. The old town is not without its open spaces, such as the cobbled and tree-lined Grassmarket.

Looming on the horizon is Arthur's Seat, an extinct volcano. Here are the Salisbury Crags, and Duddingston, a little village by a loch which is a bird sanctuary

As might be expected in a city which attracts many international visitors, there are all-year-round entertainments comprising theatre and concerts, folk music, poetry readings, exhibitions, films and jazz. Many people visit the city for the

Edinburgh International Festival, when sight-seeing becomes a welcome diversion from the surfeit of cultural events laid on during the three weeks at the end of August and early September. The Festival has an exhaustive and exhausting 'fringe' with so many features offered that 'fringe marathons' are now a popular game. One can easily suffer from cultural indigestion.

The variety of eating places in the city seems to be endless. Many offer ethnic foods, such as the *Anatolian*, in Dalry Road, for excellent Turkish fare; *Shamiana*, on Brougham Street, for Indian dishes; *Loon Fung*, on Warriston Place, for Chinese food; and *Cosmos*, North Castle Street, for Italian. A copy of *The Edinburgh Pub Guide* lets you into a few secret drinking places in the city, particularly those offering either an authentic atmosphere or some excellent drinking of real ale or malt whiskies.

Stirling

Tourist Information Centre
Dumbarton Road, tel 5019

Population 38,638

Theatre
MacRobert Arts Centre, University of Stirling

Cinema
Allan Park Entertainment Centre

Places of Interest
Stirling Castle. The castle dates mainly from the fifteenth century, but has older associations, going back to King Arthur.

Church of the Holy Rude, Broad Street. The church dates from the fifteenth century and is a fine Gothic building with impressive architecture and a unique timber roof.

The Cross, Broad Street. The spot where in 1571 Archbishop Hamilton was tried and hanged on the same day.

The Tolbooth, Broad Street. Built in 1701.

Argyll's Lodging, Castle Wynd. This was built in 1632 by Sir William Alexander, who founded Nova Scotia in 1621. In 1799 the building was used as a military hospital. It is now a youth hostel.

Outside Stirling:

The Wallace Monument. On top of Abbey Craig, built in 1869 to commemorate Scotland's first national hero William Wallace (thirteenth century). It contains an exhibition which includes the two-handed sword of Robert the Bruce.

Cambuskenneth Abbey. Just east of Stirling. Founded in 1140, it has in its time been used for sessions of Scotland's old parliament. It is now in ruins, but has an impressive fourteenth-century tower, since restored with some interesting exhibits.

Bannockburn Memorial. Two miles south of Stirling. This is the site of the Battle of Bannockburn (1314) when the English army was routed by the Scots led by Robert the Bruce. The area is now in the care of the National Trust for Scotland who run an excellent audio-visual information centre.

Because of its location in central Scotland, Stirling tends to be omitted from holiday planning as a suitable base. Yet to ignore Stirling for the sake of the east and west of Scotland would be a great pity, for the town, its immediate environs and its hinterland are all a source of great interest, not only scenically but from the area's association with many of the great events of Scotland's historical past. Stirling is within striking distance of the rambling Ochil and Lennox Hills and also is within easy access to the more muted parts of the southern Highlands.

The town is fully serviced by road and rail links. Much is on offer in the way of entertainments. The University, in particular The MacRobert Centre, has established itself as a centre for poetry readings, summer schools (devoted to all aspects of Scotland's culture), orchestral concerts and theatre. Each May Stirling mounts a Festival Fortnight during which performances in music, drama and art exhibitions are of an international standard.

Stirling Castle

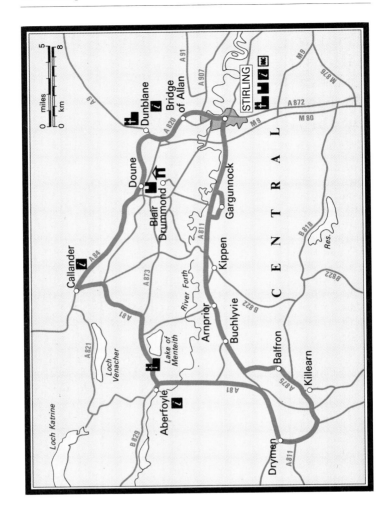

key

⊥ Church

⌂ House or Gardens

■ Castle

⌐ Archaeological Site

⋙ Viewpoint

i Tourist Information Centre

A̲A̲ AA Service Centre

R̲A̲C̲ RAC Service Centre

▮ Lighthouse

Stirling – Gargunnock – Kippen – Arnprior – Buchlyvie – Balfron – Killearn – Aberfoyle – Lake of Menteith – Callander – Doune – Blair Drummond – Dunblane – Bridge of Allan – Stirling

Tour length 60 miles

This tour is an example of how quickly one can leave a busy town and find oneself in a varied and interesting countryside. From fertile farmland the ground gradually rises to take one into some of the most beautiful areas in Scotland, where mountains, rather than dominating the scene, lend their character as a backcloth to glens, moorland and lochs. Forests, too, add their own special dimension. But the tour is not all scenery. Wherever there are villages, something of Scotland's past confronts one, from old churches, castles and monuments to magnificent Dunblane Cathedral. And a touch of the exotic is added by the Safari Park at Blair Drummond, making this trip one to remember.

Gargunnock The A811 runs westward out of Stirling, and after about 5 miles a turn-off to the left will take one to sixteenth-century Gargunnock House, with gardens open to the public. It was here that Frederick Chopin stayed when on a visit to Scotland and composed the 'Schottishe' for Miss Gargunnock, the daughter of the house. Back on the A811 another turn-off to the left (B822) **Kippen** reaches the pretty village of Kippen with an attractive church.

Arnprior The A811 is rejoined by taking the B8037 after which Arnprior is reached in a few minutes. It stands at a cross-roads, from where a short drive up the B8034 takes us to Cardross and Flanders Moss.

Buchlyvie Buchlyvie is another typical small village, where a large house is now used as a training college for the missionaries of St Patrick's Missions. From here trained priests go to African and South American charges.

Balfron Yet another small village, Balfron, is reached by taking the left turn (A875). The name (meaning 'Town of Sorrow') is said to date from when all the children were attacked and eaten by wolves. These animals were common in Scotland up until the eighteenth century when the last of the species was killed in Sutherland.

Killearn   South of Balfron is Killearn, a pretty straggling village where an obelisk commemmorates George Buchanan, a man larger than life in his times (1506–82) and who was a tutor to King James VI of Scotland. From here the A834 continues to **Drymen** join the A809 to strike northward to Drymen, a quiet pleasant spot.

Aberfoyle   The A811 now joins the A81 into Aberfoyle, nestling at the foot of the Menteith Hills. This area is famed for its scenic beauty, but also because of its associations with Rob Roy Macgregor and the settings of the novels of Sir Walter Scott (*Rob Roy* and *The Lady of the Lake*). There are mountains, woods and lochs here which is a justified excuse, if one be needed, to pause a while and stretch one's legs. Aberfoyle is a pleasant holiday village which serves as a gateway to the Trossachs and is thus popular with tourists. The entrance to the ruined church is flanked by mort-safes which gave protection against body-snatchers in the eighteenth century to the newly-buried.

Continuing along the A81 one soon reaches the **Lake of** Lake of Menteith. On an island are the ruins of **Menteith** Inchmahome Priory (ferry runs here) founded in 1238. After the political trouble which fermented after Mary, Queen of Scots, was born, the priory was used to keep her in safety (she was then aged 5) for a time before she was removed to France. There are thirteenth-century tombs here along with a recent one: that of 'Don Roberto', R B Cunninghame-Graham, Scottish author, traveller, a 'gaucho' in South America and politician. He was one of those larger than life characters who seem to dominate the Scottish scene every so often.

We now continue on the A81, past its junction **Callander** with the A873, to reach Callander. This is yet another village situated in a magnificent setting whose popularity with tourists is seen in the large number of hotels and guest-houses. The quality of service to visitors is excellent as one might expect. If one's interest in life tends towards good food, it would be no bad thing to try the *Lubnaig Hotel* (Leny Feus, just before leaving Callander), which has been awarded the AA Guesthouse of the Year accolade. It would be useful perhaps to book ahead for dinner. If time allows, one can take advantage of some of the short walks to invigorate both mind and body. The Bracklinn Falls (River Keltie) can be recommended, which is about a mile east of Callander and is located by well-marked paths.

Doune   Leaving Callander, the road is now the A84 eastward towards Doune, running through varied scenery, with to the left Braes of Boune. Also on the left, before Doune is reached, there is Doune Castle, one of the best preserved examples of Scottish fourteenth-century military/domestic architecture. At times the castle served as a royal palace, and the rooms and halls display this long historical association. The castle and its environs will repay an extended visit. A visit to Doune Park Gardens and the Doune Motor Museum should not be overlooked. The latter has a collection of historic cars, most of which are in running order.

Blair Drummond   For something different, a visit to Blair Drummond Safari Park presents an interesting diversion. Animals on show include lions, tigers, giraffes, chimps and hippos. The Park is just to the north of the main road A84, south of Callander, and from there it is a good clear run into Stirling. On the other hand, if one takes the

Dunblane   A820 into Dunblane, a different aspect is presented, mainly in the marvellous Dunblane Cathedral. Dating from the thirteenth century, the cathedral has some quite superb architectural features. The houses round the building date from the seventeenth to the nineteenth centuries, and complement the grandeur of the cathedral.

Bridge of Allan   The A9 out of Dunblane runs through Bridge of Allan, a quiet residental town, once known for its saline waters (Well House, near *Allan Water Hotel*). South of the town can be seen the buildings of the modern Stirling University. A short run ends this tour at Stirling.

Dunfermline

Tourist Information Centre
Glen Bridge Car Park, tel 20999

Population 52,057

Theatre
Carnegie Hall, Eastport

Cinema
The Cinema, Eastport

Places of Interest
Dunfermline Abbey. The nave is a relic of the church begun in 1128.
From that date various phases of building were added until 1887, when
the south-west tower was rebuilt after the original had been struck by
lightning. The grave of Robert the Bruce is in the choir, under a
memorial brass slab. During excavations in 1818, a body was
discovered wrapped in a shroud interlaced with gold threads and
encased in two lead coverings, and it was identified as that of the king.
It was reburied and covered by the present brass plate.

Pittencrieff Park. A large and extensive wooded estate with grassland,
now provided with a small zoo, apiary and specialised plant gardens.
The park was bought and gifted to the town by Andrew Carnegie, who,
as a lad, had once been barred from the estate. A fine revenge!

Pittencrieff House. A town mansion dating from 1610 which now houses
a museum devoted to local history.

Carnegie Museum, Moodie Street. The birthplace of Carnegie is now
restored and devoted to the life and work of this giant of American
industrial entrepreneurs.

Central Library, Abbot Street. It contains a collection of relics of
Robert Burns.

Folk Museum, Viewfield Terrace.

The royal burgh of Dunfermline is perhaps second only to
Edinburgh in its direct links with Scotland's past stretching
back more than a thousand years. Here many royal kings of
Scots were born, and here many of them are buried. No royal,
but a king in his own right, Andrew Carnegie, the American
industrial millionaire, was also born here. Dunfermline is clean
and pleasant and, indeed, has exactly the kind of airs and
graces which one might expect of a town proud of its past
associations. While most of Dunfermline tends to exhibit
Victorian architecture, there is much of an older age to see.
There is the magnificent Pittencrieff Park which also includes

the seventeenth-century Pittencrieff House. This is next door to the ruins of Dunfermline Abbey, which replaced Iona as the burial place of the later kings of Scotland.

Dunfermline is also an ideal centre for touring the Kingdom of Fife which, for all its association with the Scottish mining industry, is less of a 'Black Country' than one might expect to find. There are excellent rail and bus services. The entertainment facilities tend to reflect the fact that Edinburgh is only 14 miles away.

St Andrews Cathedral

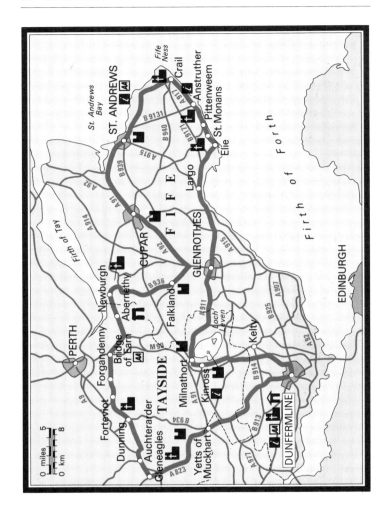

Dunfermline – Yetts o' Muchart – Gleneagles – Auchterarder – Dunning – Forteviot – Forgandenny – Bridge of Earn – Abernethy – Newburgh – Falkland – Cupar – St Andrews – Crail – Anstruther – Pittenweem – St Monans – Largo – Glenrothes – Kelty – Dunfermline

Tour length 140 miles

This tour includes parts of southern Perthshire, taking in many of the picturesque villages set in the low hills which herald the gateways to the real Highlands. Scenic changes are rung by the coastal towns of Fife where many miles of sandy beaches tempt the unwary to while away the hours. The interior of Fife is not forgotten, to introduce some interesting historical reminders of the past, and to remind one also that the area is an important mining community, often without the ugliness associated with the industry, thanks to the landscaping efforts of the National Coal Board. There are a number of surprises, too.

The A823 goes north out of Dunfermline into fairly open farming country, past the respectable heights of the Cleish Hills (to the right), to reach **Yetts o' Muchart**. This is a small village where no fewer than five roads meet. The road (A823) now strikes north through the beautiful scenery provided by **Glen Devon**, with the Ochill Hills before one. It comes as a bit of a surprise that within so short a distance of Dunfermline's city bustle there are quiet remote parts where one can relax and simply enjoy the countryside. The run through Glen Devon passes Glendevon Castle, a fifteenth-century fort which is now a public house.

From Glen Devon one passes into the wooded **Gleneagles** (Gaelic: *eaglais* – church). At the north end (near to the junction with the A9) is Gleneagles House built in 1624. The house is closed to the public, but admission is allowed by arrangement to the twelfth-century St Mungo's Chapel used by the Haldane family. Gleneagles is usually associated with the famous hotel with its equally famous golf course, often used for championship golf tournaments. Catering for the high-income bracket, the hotel is nevertheless worth visiting, if only to see how the other half lives.

Auchterarder Northward on the A9, Auchterarder lies on both sides of the highway. There are some excellent views of the hills of Strathear to the northwest. The town was burned in 1715 during the first Jacobite Rising. About 2 miles to the north, there is the Strathallan Aircraft Collection, now somewhat depleted after a recent sale of old aircraft.

A short distance north out of the village, we take the right-hand turn-off (B8062) into **Dunning** Dunning, a small village where the church boasts a twelfth-century tower. The B934 then **Forteviot** runs into Forteviot which was at one time the capital of the kings of the Picts, that race now, like the Etruscans, quite extinct except in some place-names and sculptured stones. Kenneth MacAlpin, who united the Picts and the Scots, died here in AD 860. Continuing along the B935, **Forgandenny** the road passes through Forgandenny, where the church has fragments dating from Norman times, with a belfry (c. 1600) and a rather elaborate baptismal font dating from 1744.

Bridge of Earn Bridge of Earn tends to be a dormitory suburb of Perth. The 'bridge' crosses the River Earn which flows into the upper reaches of the Firth of Tay. Take the A90 now south out of Bridge of Earn, **Abernethy** and then turn left at Abernethy, yet another settlement which was once a Pictish capital. Tradition has it that here William the Conqueror met Malcolm Canmore, the Scots king, in 1072. Now reduced to the status of a village, Abernethy still retains the visible evidence of the past, chiefly in its Round Tower, the lower part of which dates from the ninth century. It was possibly used as a bell tower at one time.

Newburgh Continuing on the A913 one reaches Newburgh, east of which are the scanty remains of Lindores Abbey, one of the great religious houses in the area until 1600. The Abbey was founded in 1191. Newburgh itself is a royal burgh with a small harbour. About $1\frac{1}{2}$ miles south of the town is

MacDuff's Cross, which was once a sanctuary for any member of the MacDuff clan who had murdered in the heat of an argument. To obtain atonement for the crime, the guilty man had to touch the Cross (now a pedestal within a circle of stones), and tie nine cows to it.

Falkland From Newburgh the A983 runs through Auchtermuchty to Falkland. This small burgh has a right royal status and is full of restored houses dating from the seventeenth to the nineteenth centuries. Add to this the town's setting at the foot of the Lomond Hills and one has a perfect spot to linger and soak in some delightful atmosphere. But there is a bonus attraction in Falkland: the sixteenth-century royal residence. Falkland Palace was begun before 1500, on the site of an earlier castle mentioned in a charter dated 1160. The palace became a favourite residence away from the Edinburgh court scene for a succession of Scottish kings. Both Charles I and II visited Falkland. In 1715 Rob Roy Macgregor occupied the palace and levied dues on the town. Perhaps the saddest event the palace saw was in 1542 when James V arrived a broken man after his defeat at Solway Moss. On his death-bed he received a visitor who told him that he was the father of a new-born daughter: Mary, Queen of Scots. On hearing the news he said: 'God's will be done; it cam wi a lass and it'll gang wi a lass'. That prophecy came true eventually when the Stewarts lost their claim to the throne of Great Britain. A visitor centre is run by the National Trust for Scotland and visits through the Palace are by guided tours only. The garden has been replanted according to an old print design and includes the Royal Tennis Court (1539). If there is time for a bite to eat, reports are favourable of the Scottish fare in *Kind Kyttock's Kitchen.*

Cupar The A912 runs south to cross-roads where one now picks up the A92 to Cupar, passing through some of the richest arable farmland in Scotland. Cupar is of ancient lineage, but its past has virtually disappeared, with possibly the parish church, whose tower dates from 1415, standing a lone witness to the past. There are, however, several interesting places to visit around the town. Dalgairn House Garden is rather unusual in that its display is devoted to 'weeds' and old-fashioned plants, reflecting how much modern medicine is reliant on modern drugs rather than the old herbal remedies. Scotstarvit Tower, a little south of the town, dates from 1579 and opposite is the mansion Hill of Tarvit, a 1906 copy of a 1696 building. Now a convalescent home, it houses a collection of paintings and furniture, tapestry and porcelain.

St Andrews   A drive of 10 miles takes us on to the northern Fife coast and into the ancient town of St Andrews, famous for its university and the golf course. One is conscious of rubbing shoulders with the Middle Ages as one walks the streets of this old town, off which many narrow wynds run. The houses here have long gardens, called 'riggs', which are still intact after 500 years. The university, founded in 1411, is the oldest seat of learning of Scotland. The castle, now in ruins overlooking a rocky shore out to the North Sea, dates from 1200 and has a bloody history. In only one incident of many Cardinal Beaton was murdered here in 1546 by a number of religious reformers who then barricaded themselves in the castle (being joined by John Knox) for a year until their siege was broken by French and Scots ships. The reformers were then sent to France and forced to become galley slaves.

St Andrew's Cathedral is also in a ruinous state, but still retains an impressive dignity. Many of the stones from the old building were incorporated as building material in some of the town's older houses. The Royal and Ancient Golf Club is at the northern end of the town. It was founded in 1754, since when the sport has spread around the world. All four courses are open to the public.

Crail   The A917 is never far from the sea as it runs out of St Andrews and south into Crail, the first of a string of ancient fishing towns on the Forth estuary coast of Fife. Created a royal burgh in 1310 by King Robert the Bruce, it has many of the architectural delights which link it firmly with its past. Credit is due to the National Trust for Scotland for its work of restoration in the town. Delightful buildings catch the eye at nearly every turn. The harbour is often busy with boats landing catches of the far-famed Crail lobsters. At the east of the town is the sixteenth-century Collegiate Church of St Mary, which includes parts of an earlier twelfth-century building. A visit to the local Museum (in Marketgate) repays the time spent there.

Anstruther   Four miles along the coast is Anstruther (pronounced 'Enster'), another fishing village, again a delight just to wander around. It was a centre for herring fishing until the 1940s. It is now the home of the Scottish Fisheries Museum, housed in a cluster of buildings dating from the sixteenth century. The whole display is devoted to the history of the Scottish fishing industry and includes real craft, models and tableaux. The

Pittenweem   next village is Pittenweem which, like Anstruther, is closely tied to the sea. At the eastern end of the harbour is a group of restored sixteenth-century houses called The Gyles. The parish church, at the eastern end of High Street, has a sixteenth-century tower. In its time Pittenweem was a trading centre with the Continent and many of its buildings reflect the style of the gentry of two centuries ago.

St Monans   Next along the coast of the Firth of Forth is St Monans, well known in the industry for its 200-year-old boat-building expertise. Visit the fourteenth-century Church of St Monan, still used for worship after 600 years. The town itself is a delight with the red-tiled roofs of houses catching the eye at every turn. The little village

Elie   of Elie is a popular holiday resort, with attrac-
Largo   tive and extensive sands. Largo is really two towns, Upper and Lower, and are about a mile apart. Lower Largo is the birthplace of Alexander Selkirk, perhaps better known as Robinson Crusoe. He is remembered in a statuette above the door of the 300-year-old cottage where he was born.

From Largo the A915 continues to join the A911
Glenrothes   into Glenrothes, now a 'new town' development designed to attract light industry to replace the older coal-mining industry. The road now goes north to skirt the top shore of Loch Leven and

Milnathort   into Milnathort. This is a little village close by Burleigh Castle, a sixteenth-century ruin, beyond which are some standing stones.

The A911 out of Milnathort becomes the B996
Kinross running into Kinross, lying on the western shore
of Loch Leven. The town has some interesting
sights, including the seventeenth-century
Tolbooth. The Museum in High Street is devoted
to local history and has exhibits on linen and
peat. A ferry from Kinross will take the visitor
Loch Leven across Loch Leven to Loch Leven Castle, from
which Mary, Queen of Scots escaped after being
imprisoned there in 1567. The loch is a National
Nature Reserve and is an important breeding
ground for many varieties of wildfowl, including
pink-foot and grey-lag geese. The route back to
Kelty Dunfermline is through Kelty, a typical Fife
mining community, surrounded by reminders of
the old days when the miner was virtually a slave
to his trade.

Perth

Tourist Information Centre
The Round House, Marshall Place, tel 22900

Population 41,998

Theatre
Perth Theatre, High Street

Cinemas
Odeon, Kinnoull Street
Playhouse, Murray Street

Places of Interest
St John's Kirk, John Street. The church was originally founded in 1126, but now displays Gothic architecture dating from the sixteenth century. The choir has its original wooden roof. The whole of the interior is quietly impressive.

Fair Maid's House. This medieval building behind Charlotte Street is one of the oldest in Perth. It got its name from the novel by Sir Walter Scott in which he describes the clan combat which took place in 1396 at the North Inch.

North Inch. Now a park containing the domed Bell Sports Centre. It was a rallying point for the Jacobites in the 1715 and 1745 Risings.

Museum and Art Gallery. At the western end of the old Perth Bridge. It contains displays of local history and has a number of utensils and equipment used in the early days of whisky making.

Balhousie Castle. A fine building, off Hay Street, built in 1478 and later restored. It now houses the Regimental Museum of the Black Watch, formed in 1739.

Branklyn Gardens, Dundee Road. The gardens contain many rare plants from all parts of the world.

Scone Palace. About a mile north of Perth, the palace dates from the early eighteenth century and contains magnificent collections of French furniture and porcelain, ivories and sixteenth-century needlework. Part of the palace has a 400-year-old wooden floor from an earlier building on the site.

The 'Fair City' of Perth is often called the 'Gateway to the Highlands' for it is through Perth the traveller must pass to gain access to the grandeur of the Grampian Mountains and, farther north, the beautiful desolation of north-west Sutherland. Much of the beauty of Perth is due to the fact that it lies on both sides of the River Tay, and it is this setting which must have influenced those whose wealth enabled many impressive buildings to grace the city. As a focal point in the very heart of Scotland, Perth boasts a network of communications which includes road, rail and air. The Information Centre is a converted nineteenth-century waterworks, now known as the Round House. It has a unique 360° slide audio-visual programme showing the attractions of Perth and its environs. The Victorian *Perth Theatre* is the longest established in Scotland.

Perth used to be the capital of Scotland, though little of its ancient lineage remains. Much was destroyed in the sixteenth century, during the turbulent times of religious division, promoted by the fiery preaching of the reformer John Knox in St John's Kirk in 1559. Even so, recent archaeological 'digs' are revealing up to 1,500 years of continuous occupation. Some parts of the city have a 'hang-dog' look, the result of civic neglect; but, strangely, this aspect has a kind of fascination with an atmosphere which conjures up something of the past.

Apart from being a major tourist centre, Perth is also a commercial and industrial city. Whisky, insurance, textiles and dye-works are all here, the latter still seen in the impressive mill established by Sir John Pullar soon after the discovery of the first aniline dyestuff known as 'Perkin's Mauve' the commercial possibilities of which Sir John was not so slow to exploit. The best overview of the city is from Kinnoull Hill, provided with a Nature Trail and about 40 minutes' walk from the station (across the Perth Bridge). From here also one can see the surrounding countryside and the hills which gradually increase in height towards the north to melt into the Grampians.

Perth – Methven – Fowlis Wester – Crieff – Comrie – St Fillans – Lochearnhead – Balquidder – Killin – Fortingall – Aberfeldy – Smaa Glen – Perth

Tour length 110 miles

This tour is largely scenic, taking the visitor into the central Highlands where hills overlook broad green straths, and into the country of Rob Roy Macgregor. Lochs Earn and Tay provide breathtaking vistas and welcome chances to stop and simply soak in the beauty of green fields, woodlands, rust-coloured moorland and trim villages which almost merge unnoticed into their surroundings.

The A85 goes north out of Perth and then turns west. Just after leaving the city boundary, to the right, is Huntingtower Castle, a fifteenth-century castellated mansion, or rather two medieval tower-houses connected by later seventeenth-century work. The impressive wooden ceiling and walls in the original hall are certainly worth viewing. It was the scene in 1582 of the 'Ruthven Raid' in which the young King James VI of Scotland was captured by conspirators and imprisoned here.

Methven   The A85 continues through the village of Methven, where the fragmentary ruins of a fifteenth-century church can be seen. Just to the north of Methven Robert the Bruce was defeated in a battle with the English in 1306. Farther on,

Fowlis Wester   another small village called Fowlis Wester is reached up a turn to the right, with associations which span some 1,200 years. Here is the church of St Bean, dating from the thirteenth century but built on the site of the former chapel erected by St Bean (died c. 720). There is a Pictish stone here which was discovered embedded in the wall of the church. The modern aspect comes from the fact that astronaut Alan Bean took with him to the moon a piece of the MacBean tartan, a section of which was donated to the church. There is a photographic display of moon pictures.

Crieff   The first major town on this route is Crieff. In

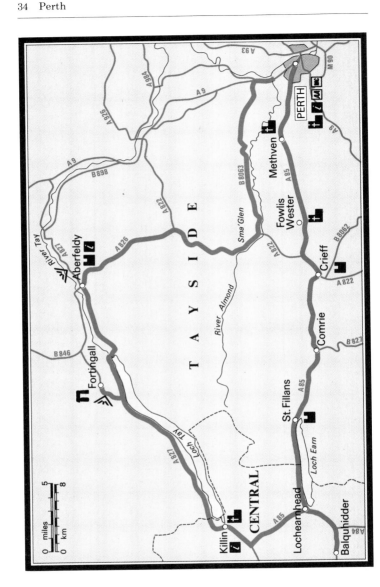

the eighteenth and nineteenth centuries, it was a 'tryst' or market town for cattle. Drovers from all over the Highlands took weeks and sometimes months to drive cattle from as far away as the Hebrides to sell their beasts to the highest bidders from England who were often contracted to supply the British army and navy. Situated on the slopes of the Knock (Gaelic: *cnoc*, a hill) of Crieff and close to the River Earn, Crieff is now a popular tourist centre. In the earlier years of this century, it was regarded as a health resort, indicating the physical and mental stimulation one obtained from the town's locality. At the entrance to the Town Hall (High Street) there is the Cross (seventeenth century) of the Burgh of Regality of Drummond (Crieff's former name) and a little farther on an older cross, the tenth-century Mercat Cross. The Museum on Lodge Street is devoted to local history. Fine glass hand-blown objects are produced at Stuart Strathearn on Muthill Road. About two miles south of Crieff is Drummond Castle, founded in 1491 and the scene of sieges in the seventeenth and eighteenth centuries, when the castle was partly demolished. It was later restored, with the Italian-style gardens particularly attractive, being laid out in terraces.

Comrie The A85 proceeds west out of Crieff through typical Perthside countryside to Comrie. This is an interesting village for a number of reasons. First, it sits on a geological fault which produces the occasional earth tremor but nothing to worry about! Secondly, Comrie houses the Museum of Scottish Tartans which has a record of over 1,300 tartans and which dispels many of the fanciful beliefs about tartan. Tartan weaving is a live demonstration in the museum, and an adjoining garden contains the plants grown in the old days to produce dyes of various hues used in the design of tartan. The Comrie Smiddy Museum is devoted to exhibits from bygone times.

St Fillans From Comrie the road skirts the northern shore of beautiful Loch Earn, just before which is the village of St Fillans where one can see the ruins of a fifteenth-century chapel, built on the site of the old religious cell of St Fillan, who was reputed to be able to cure insanity. Loch Earn itself is a narrow 7-mile stretch of water, at the foot of impressive mountains whose slopes run gently down to the water's edge. At the western end of the loch is the village of Lochearnhead, the base for many water sports and sailing facilities.

Lochearnhead

A short diversion is now recommended. Take the A84 south and turn to the right at Kingshouse for Balquidder. In the churchyard are the tombs of Rob Roy Macgregor and his family. The Clan Macgregor was outlawed in the fifteenth century for atrocities ascribed to them and for which they were not wholly blameless. Members of the clan were forced by law to adopt other surnames, a situation which was not resolved until centuries later. Rob Roy himself was a freebooter who became 'respectable' and whose exploits were immortalised by the novel by Sir Walter Scott. The church (nineteenth century) contains a number of ancient relics, including an eighth-century sculptured stone.

Balquidder

Retracing the road back to Lochearnhead, we pick up the A85 to go northward to the crossroads where the road becomes the A827 which takes us into Killin. This is but one of many charming villages met on this route, with white-washed houses, in a sylvan setting and with the mountains forming an impressive backcloth. It lies at the western end of Loch Tay. Killin church, rebuilt in 1744, is thought to have been in use in the ninth century. The baptismal font is 1,000 years old and is the only seven-sided example of its kind in Scotland. At the entrance to Killin are the Falls of Dochart, where the waters tumble over each other on the way to Loch Tay. In the River Dochart are two islets, one of which is the burial ground of the Clan MacNab, the main clan in the area until they emigrated to Canada in 1823. Just north out of Killin is Finlarig Castle, now ruins which tell little of its history as the seat of a branch of Clan Campbell, Black Duncan of Cowal, who ruled with the power of the 'pit and the gallows' in arbitrary justice. Close by is a beheading pit, the only one of its kind surviving in Scotland.

Killin

The A827 makes its way along the northern shore of Loch Tay. The first turning on the left goes up a side road into the Ben Lawers Nature Reserve, where an Information Centre offers comprehensive facts about the area. At Fearnan, another left turn up a minor road reaches the

Fortingall village of Fortingall. The yew tree in the churchyard is said to be 3,000 years old and shows its age. Four terraced cottages in the village were once thatched but now have slated roofs after a fire in 1979. They are still rather attractive, with their arched dormers. Fortingall is reputed to be the birthplace of Pontius Pilate, born at a Roman camp established in the village area during the Roman occupation of Britain. The hill fort behind the village was once occupied by a local kinglet. This tradition relating to Pilate has puzzled many and yet there is some evidence that it has an element of truth in it. It is suggested that Pilate was sent to Rome as a boy slave and taken into the Roman family of the Pontii, later to be given a 'pilateus', the felt cap worn by a free slave. His marriage to Claudia Procula, the illegitimate grand-daughter of Emperor Tiberius, gave him access to rank and promotion, and ultimately the Governorship of Judea in AD26. After his fall from grace ten years later he vanished from Roman records. But it has been suggested that he returned to Fortingall to die here. Was it coincidence that a stone burial slab was discovered at the turn of this century bearing the initials 'PP'? The meaning of Fortingall is 'Fort of the Strangers'.

Leaving Fortingall, the A846 is picked up to pass through Dull, the site of an early Christian centre later transferred to St Andrews in Fife and the origin of St Andrews University. The founder of Dull was Mansuteus, who, it is suggested, took the disgraced Pilate back to Fortingall, the latter to end his days in some kind of disturbed peace.

Just before Aberfeldy on the left is Castle Menzies, a sixteenth-century Z-plan towerhouse which houses the Clan Menzies museum.

Aberfeldy Aberfeldy is another popular tourist centre and has been since it was visited by Robert Burns in 1787 and the beauty of the surrounding scenery immortalised in his song *The Birks of Aberfeldy* (Birks: silver birch). Among the 'sights' is the bridge built by General Wade, the inveterate builder of roads in the eighteenth century which opened up the Highlands. The Aberfeldy bridge, which is quite the finest Wade designed, was erected in 1733. Nearby is a large cairn surmounted by a kilted figure which commemmorates the raising of the Black Watch regiment in 1739 (the cairn was erected in 1887). A visit to the Oatmeal Mill in Mill Street will be rewarded by seeing how raw grain is changed into fine oatmeal.

One now returns to Perth *via* the south-going Glen Cochill, the Smaa Glen and Glen Almond (taking the A826, the A822 and the B8063). This is mainly a scenic run and provides a pleasant and *Smaa Glen* relaxing finish to the day's touring. The Smaa Glen is one of the gateways to the Highlands and was used by the 1745 Jacobites on their retreat from the south. After the Battle of Culloden, General Wade then got to work on making the road. At the southern end of the Smaa Glen, the left turn-off is the B8063, a short distance along which, at Buchanty, is the Buchanty Spout – in fact rapids on the River Almond and a famous salmon leap in due season. Thereafter the B8063 joins the main A9 into Perth.

Pitlochry

Tourist Information Centre
28 Atholl Road, tel 2215

Population 2,610

Theatre
Pitlochry Festival Theatre, Lower Oakfield

Cinema
Regal, West Moulin Road

Places of Interest
Pitlochry Festival Theatre

Eighth-century Pictish Cross slab. Across the Tummel at Dunfallandy, close to Logierait Road beyond caravan site.

Salmon fish pass. At hydro-electric dam at Loch Faskally, with observation chamber and exhibition room.

Black Spout. A waterfall $1\frac{1}{2}$ miles south of the town.

If ever a town found itself in a favoured spot for attracting visitors it is Pitlochry. Set in quite dramatic and varied scenery and located at the foot of the Grampian mountains, with the River Tummel as a bonus attraction, Pitlochry's popularity is seen in the numbers of tourists who make the town the centre for sampling the surrounding countryside of forests and lochs. It might come as a surprise to some to realise that Pitlochry boasts a major Scottish theatre. Now housed in a magnificent building, it started off life literally in a tent. The town was originally established as a commercial centre and once had a number of woollen textile mills. Nowadays tourism is the major element in its economic base and the population swells considerably in the summer months. It is on the main road from Perth to Inverness and is served by the railway line between these points.

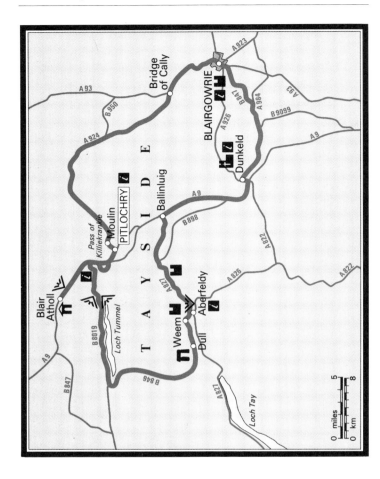

Pitlochry – Moulin – Bridge of Cally – Blairgowrie – Dunkeld – Ballinluig – Weem – Dull – Loch Tummel – Killiecrankie – Blair Atholl – Pitlochry

Tour length 90 miles

This tour takes in some of the scenery which is claimed to be second to none in Scotland, from the fertile Carse of Gowrie in the east, to the magnificent scenery in the west of loch, moorland, forest and mountain. Two highlights are the seat of the Dukes of Atholl at Blair Castle, and the impressive cathedral at Dunkeld. Inevitably, some of Scotland's past looms up in places, but is now mellowed with the passage of the years. Even so, these historic places still manage to convey an appropriate atmosphere and become almost real events in imaginative minds.

Moulin The A924 goes east out of Pitlochry to pass through the delightful and charming village of Moulin. The church here was rebuilt in 1874 on a site which has been devoted to Christian worship for many centuries. A short distance away are the ruins of Castle Dubh (thirteenth century). In 1500 the men in the castle were struck by plague and in an effort to contain the disease, the building was battered down by cannon. It now forms a doleful cairn for the men of the garrison. A path behind *Moulin Hotel* will take one up an easy climb to the top of Craigower Hill, from where one can take in the magnificent vista westward towards Strath Tummel.

Bridge of Cally Out of Moulin the road goes through Glen Brerachan and then turns southward into Strathardle to Bridge of Cally. All here is well cared-for countryside and one can sense some-thing of the pride of the caretakers of nature's delights in well-tended fields and tree-lined narrow roads. Bridge of Cally (it spans the River Ericht) is a peaceful place with its bracing air one of its more attractive features.

Blairgowrie The A93 road from Braemar is joined at Bridge of Cally and runs south into Blairgowrie. At one time this town had flax and jute mills, but these are now idle. Prosperity is today based on raspberries. In 1898 a local man was so impressed with the quality of wild raspberries growing in the area that he started to grow the fruit as a commercial crop. Since then the climate, soil and altitude have all combined to make the area one of the major fruit-growing districts in the British Isles. There are three castles within easy reach of the town: ruined Clascune, 2 miles on a hill to the north-west; Newton (seventeenth century) situated high above the town; and Ardblair, a sixteenth-century fortified house haunted by a Green Lady. It houses mementoes of Lady Caroline Nairne who wrote such popular Jacobite songs as *Charlie is my Darling*.

Out of Blairgowrie on the A93, the B947 is picked up by taking the turning to the right, and then joining up with the A984, to pass through the tiny settlements of Spitalfield and Caputh into Dunkeld.

Dunkeld

A few places situated along the Highland Boundary Fault line (a kind of San Andreas fault) claim to be the 'Gateway to the Highlands'. Dunkeld, however, seems best to deserve the name. Here the River Tay breaks through a gap in the wooded hills to create a natural gate. Dunkeld's main feature is the cathedral, which is rather appropriate since Dunkeld was the site of a monastery founded by St Adamnan, the biographer of St Columba of Iona, before AD700. Dunkeld was also a Pictish capital. The present village takes its ancient historical associations seriously, as witness the results of recent renovations of the 'Little Houses' (Cathedral Street), eighteenth-century buildings which are now a delight to the eye.

Though it is now roofless, there is a quiet dignity within the powerful walls of the Dunkeld cathedral. Some parts of the building date from the twelfth century, but most date from the fourteenth and fifteenth. Indeed the NW tower was completed in 1501, just 60 years before the cathedral was the focus of the attention of Scottish religious reformers in 1650, who were responsible for the destruction of the cathedral. Neglect in later centuries, including the removal of the leaded roof, gave nature the chance to complete the work of ruin. In the parish kirk end of the cathedral (restored in 1908) there is a monument to Alexander Stewart, the Wolf of Badenoch, who destroyed Elgin Cathedral. After doing penance for this deed, his body was allowed to be buried within the sanctuary of holy ground.

The bridge across the Tay at Dunkeld was built by Telford in 1809. Across the river is Birnam, made famous by Shakespeare (in *Macbeth*) because it was the trees of Birnam Wood which moved to Dunsinane, some 11 miles away, and which heralded the end of Macbeth.

Ballinluig Leaving the green swards beside Dunkeld Cathedral, the A9 is taken north to Ballinluig, where the waters of the rivers Tay and Tummel meet. West out of the village runs the A827 to follow the River Tay, passing through a number of small settlements including Logierait, where in olden times the Duke of Atholl administered rough arbitrary justice to wrongdoers. Rob Roy Macgregor was once incarcerated in the gaol here, but he managed to escape to enjoy further exploits, pitting his wits against the kind of law and order that existed then. This road runs through Aberfeldy and then strikes north (B846)

Weem past Weem where the sixteenth-century Castle Menzies is a fine example of a Scottish Z-plan tower-house. It houses the Clan Menzies museum. The B846 now runs through the pleas-

Dull ant countryside of Appin of Dull. At Dull there is a cluster of four standing stones and, in the village itself, a seventh-century Celtic cross.

Tummel Bridge lies at the western end of Loch Tummel, where we now strike eastward (B8019).

Loch Tummel Loch Tummel lies on the famous 'Road to the Isles', *via* Loch Rannoch and Lochaber to the island in the far west. The road skirts the north shore of Loch Tummel, through dense woodland. At the eastern end of the loch is the Loch Tummel Forest Centre, where the Forestry Commission has created a centre to interpret the history and ecology of the area for visitors. While here, enjoy the 'Queen's view', from where a magnificent view is obtained up Loch Tummel to the conical peak of Schiehallion. This view is named after Queen Victoria who was so entranced with the scenery. But there is a tradition that Mary, Queen of Scots also was charmed with the view on one of her visits to the area.

Killiecrankie   The B8019 now joins the A9 at the Pass of Killiecrankie. At this place in 1689 a battle was fought between the English troops of King William and the Jacobite Highlanders, in which the latter won the day under the leadership of Bonnie Dundee. The Visitor Centre here is run by the National Trust for Scotland, and has an audio-visual display explaining, in considerable detail, the events which led up to the battle. The actual pass is a narrow gorge through which both road and railway thread their way. Tracks lead down through oak trees into the gorge where one can view the famous 'Soldier's Leap', a gap of some 18 feet across which an English soldier managed to escape from pursuing Highlanders after the battle.

Blair Atholl   A few miles up the A9 is Blair Atholl, a small village and the last of any size before the A9 makes its way across the moorland to the north. The main attraction here is Blair Castle, a large white-harled Scottish baronial mansion. It stands at a strategic position: at the meeting of the old roads from the south and Deeside, *via* Glen Tilt. The oldest part of the castle dates from about 1270, since when various additions were made up to 1904. The castle has seen much of Scotland's history played out within and outside its walls. In 1746 it was besieged by the Jacobites and is the very last castle in the British Isles to have been in this situation. The castle is the home of the Duke of Atholl, who is the only British subject allowed to retain a private army.

Inside the castle there is a veritable fairyland of treasures, from tapestry and furniture to weapons, the collection here being one of the best in Scotland. Individual displays are devoted to the natural history of the area, and to Georgian and Victorian toys. Be prepared to spend some time viewing these extensive collections. Indeed there is so much to be seen in the castle that one might well decide to be selective after consulting the guide book.

From Blair Atholl, it is now a short run south on the A9 back into Pitlochry.

Dundee

Population 174,746

Theatres
Dundee Repertory, 113 Lochee Road
Little, 58 Victoria Road
Whitehall, Bellfield Street

Cinemas
ABC, Seagate
Odeon, Cowgate
Tivoli, Bonnybank Road
Victoria, Victoria Road

Places of Interest
The Old Steeple, Nethergate. St Mary's Tower dates from the fifteenth century and is all that remains of an earlier twelfth-century church. It contains a display of the religious history of the city.

The Howff, Meadowside. An ancient burial ground used for 300 years and containing a collection of memorials of the sixteenth to eighteenth centuries second in Scotland only to Greyfriars in Edinburgh.

Dudhope Castle, Dudhope Park. Built in the thirteenth century to replace the earlier Dundee Castle, it has undergone many changes.

Albert Institute, Albert Square. It contains the Central Museum and Art Gallery, with the Scottish school of painting a particular feature.

Spalding Golf Museum, Camperdown Park. Interesting for those whose minds wish to go back to the very first tee!

Barrack Street Museum, Ward Road. Exhibits relate to ships built in or associated with the city.
H.M.S. Unicorn, Victoria Dock. This is the oldest British warship still afloat; launched in 1824 she has been restored to her original condition.

Outside Dundee:

Broughty Castle. On a spit of land at Broughty Ferry, a continuation of Dundee. Completed in 1496, it is now a museum.

Claypotts Castle. Also in Broughty Ferry. The earliest mention of the castle is in the sixteenth century. It has been well restored and is the most complete tower-house of its kind in Scotland.

Dundee is Scotland's fourth largest city. Its associations with the past have been centred on industrial and commercial activities. Although much of 'old Dundee' has disappeared, what has replaced it has created a fine looking city with a tasteful blending of modern and Victorian styles of architecture. Its prosperity has made it a busy city where the noise of traffic is something one tends to get used to. Travel services are comprehensive and include rail, bus and air links.

Evidence that Dundee has been a 'desirable residential area' for many thousands of years has been found in the city's Stannergate, where a prehistoric kitchen midden was discovered late last century. Since these early times, the settlement has grown into a city of major significance in the economy of Scotland. Little is known about the early history of Dundee, until the twelfth century when the city was created a royal burgh by King Willian the Lion and Dundee started to grow into a major port with valuable trading links with the Continent. One of the most important industries established in Dundee was textiles, which continued through flax and linen to jute. Dundee's association with the whaling trade of last century brought prosperity until that trade fell away with the increasing scarcity of the whale species.

Historically, Dundee is firmly embedded in the turbulent events which often wrenched Scotland apart into warring factions. In 1547 the forces of the English King Henry viii held the town for a week, during which the citizens felt the heavy hand of the occupying troops, and emerged from the experience to see their homes ablaze. About a century later it was stormed by Montrose and was treated with no less severity. Hardly had the city recovered from that assault when General Monk arrived in 1651 to mete out harsh treatment once again. Dundee was occupied by the Jacobites of the 1745 Rising, who held it for nearly a year, during which time the citizens were treated with reasonable courtesy. Later, and in more peaceful times, Dundee managed to establish itself as a centre of trade, industry and commerce. Ships from Dundee have sailed to both the Arctic and the Antarctic, the latter during the ill-fated search for the South Pole by Scott in 1910. Among the famous names associated with Dundee are Mary Shelley, who wrote the book *Frankenstein*; Mary Slessor, the African missionary; Sir Robert Watson Watt, inventor of Radar; and William McGonagall, possibly the world's best-known worst poet, whose verses are still in print.

Dundee – Coupar Angus – Meigle – Glamis – Kirriemuir – Forfar – Finavon – Brechin – Edzell – Montrose – Lunan Bay – Arbroath – Monikie – Dundee

Tour length 120 miles

The suggested route takes the visitor inland, through the fertile farmlands in Strathmore and through countryside in the foothills which hint at the mountains and moorlands of the Highlands. The scenery then changes to coastal vistas as the road runs south with the grey waters of the North Sea reminding one of the oil wealth off Scotland's shorelands. History from Scotland's turbulent past meets the visitor face to face in not a few places. Glamis Castle is possibly the highlight of this trip.

Coupar Angus The A923 runs north-west out of Dundee into the Sidlaw Hills, where the undulating countryside supports numerous small farming communities whose love for the land is seen in the carefully cultured fields and woodlands. This is a pleasant relaxing run to Coupar Angus, a market town, with rural rhythms. The town's Tolbooth dates from 1762. The museum (Cumberland Barracks) has displays of local history. Some fragmentary ruins beside the Dundee road into Coupar Angus are all that remain of a Cistercian Abbey founded in 1164 and destroyed in 1559.

Meigle Out from the town, pick up the A94 for Meigle. This little place has a museum which has a collection of about 30 sculptured stones from the seventh century to the tenth century. All these stones were originally located in the old churchyard in Meigle. They are magnificent examples of the kind of early Christian art form which incorporated Pictish symbols. Little is known about the Picts because they left no written material. But these stones, with their intricately carved tracery, indicate a highly cultured people who used symbols as some kind of code. Belmont Castle near by was once the home of Sir Henry Campbell-Bannerman, a British Prime Minister.

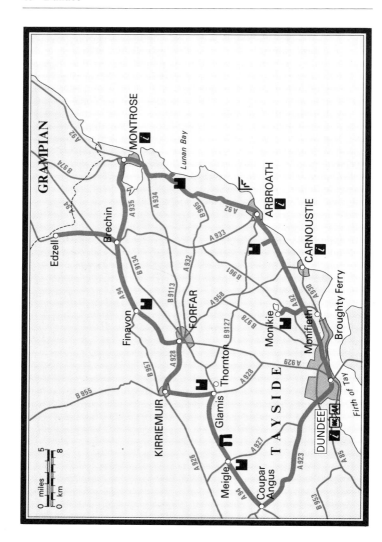

Glamis   The A94 now continues to reach Glamis (pronounced 'Glams'). The village has a Folk
Museum, set in four converted seventeenth-
century cottages, which is devoted to the domestic and agricultural lives of the people of the area
during the last 200 years. The main feature of
interest here is Glamis Castle, just north of the
village. This magnificent structure, with its
clusters of rounded turrets, dates variously from
the thirteenth to the sixteenth centuries. The
castle was the childhood home of Queen
Elizabeth, the Queen Mother, but it has many
other royal associations, going back to the first
Sir John Lyon who, in 1376, married the daughter of King Robert II of Scotland. The interior of
the castle contains enough of interest to warrant
a full day of sight-seeing. The castle grounds
include a late nineteenth-century formal garden.
Back in Glamis village, pay a visit to the Manse
of Glamis to see yet another Pictish Stone,
carved with a decorative cross on one side and
fish and serpent symbols on the other. It dates
from the ninth century and is in remarkable
condition.

The A928 leads north out of Glamis towards the
foot of the Grampian Mountains and into
Kirriemuir   Kirriemuir. Here the warmth one gets from this
friendly old town is complemented by the red
sandstone used in many of the buildings.
Kirriemuir is the birthplace of Sir J. M. Barrie,
playwright and novelist whose *Peter Pan* is
known the world over. The house in which he
was born (9 Brechin Road) is a museum devoted
to Barrie, his life and works. Kirriemuir was
once a town of weavers, which activity is
reflected in the narrow wynds which separate the
houses and in the steep streets. It is said that to
preserve their privacy, no house front door faces
that of another, which seems to explain the
haphazard nature of the houses.

A short run east down the A926 takes us into
Forfar   Forfar. This is a busy town with industry as its
main economic base. It has however an ancient
lineage, going back at least as far as 1057 when
King Malcolm Canmore used the town as a place
to hold his first Parliament. There is much in
Forfar to remind one of the past, in particular

Little Causeway, a picturesque cobbled square behind West High Street. The Town Hall (built in 1788) sports some fine paintings. The Meffan Institute houses a museum. Try one of the famous 'Forfar Bridies', a half-moon shaped pastry filled with baked meat and onions. They are truly delicious and one could easily become addicted to them.

Finavon   The A94 now heads north to Finavon. Small though this village might be, it has been a site of strategic importance, as witness the hill-forts in the area (one is on Turin Hill, a mile to the south). This importance was later taken up by the building of Finavon Castle, founded in the thirteenth century with later additions, by the Earls of Crawford. One of these earls, 'Earl Beardie', hanged his minstrel by hooks from the castle tower. His other tenants also received the unwelcome attentions of this cruel despot. Visit the Dovecot, just to the north of the A94, where over 2,000 nesting boxes for pigeons have been restored. It was used once as a living larder in the old days and still attracts birds.

The next port of call on the A94 going north is **Brechin**   Brechin. A market town for the surrounding district, it has also some industry. The main feature of interest here must be the Cathedral, which dates back to the twelfth century, beside the fine Round Tower, one of only two in Scotland, (the other is at Abernethy) and built around AD1000. Much restoration work in the cathedral has made the building one of great architectural interest, not least the tombstones dating from the tenth to the thirteenth centuries. Brechin Castle (no admission), next to the cathedral, is the home of the Earl of Dalhousie. Dating from the thirteenth century, the castle was rebuilt in 1711.

Edzell   The B966 is used for a diversion visit to Edzell, set in the strath of the North Esk River, and a claimant of the award 'The Best Kept Village in Scotland'. Edzell Castle is a tower house (sixteenth century) built of red sandstone and is adjacent to the 'pleasance', or walled garden, created by Sir David Lindsay in 1604. The arch at the southern entrance to Edzell village was erected in 1887 to the Earl of Dalhousie.

Montrose Back through Brechin, the A935 is picked up to move eastward towards Montrose. The last two miles of this road skirt the north side of the Montrose tidal basin (into which the South Esk River flows), before joining the A92 Aberdeen road into Montrose. This town has a long historical association with the North Sea. It established itself first with trade links with Scandinavia and the Low countries, then with the extensive smuggling trade which reached a peak after the Act of Union of 1707 between England and Scotland, under which luxuries such as silks and wines were imported only under strict government licence. Smugglers became wealthy supplying a black market. This no doubt has given Montrose the look of prosperity in its old buildings, but so has the present-day involvement with North Sea oil. One gets the impression that there is no time to spare for leisure in Montrose, there is so much bustle. But the visitor can in fact relax a while, if only on the extensive sandy beach. Otherwise, a look round the town will present the visitor with some fine buildings, notably the Old Church (1834) and the Old Town Hall (1763), behind which is the Museum, with displays of local interest.

Lunan Bay A 14-mile run south on the A92 takes us to another coastal town, Arbroath. But if time allows, a stop at Lunan Bay will prove interesting. This bay is a 4-mile stretch of sands, overlooked by the grim ruin of Red Castle. This fifteenth-century tower replaced an earlier stronghold designed as a defence against Danish invaders. There is a 25-foot-deep pit prison within the castle. The building was destroyed in 1579 when the lady owner had a bitter feud with her divorced husband. The cliff scenery around the bay is quite spectacular.

Arbroath The main claim to a niche in Scottish history by Arbroath is the event which took place in Arbroath Abbey in 1320. This was the signing of the Scottish Declaration of Independence, which took the form of a letter sent to Pope John XXII stating:

'For so long as there shall be but one hundred of us remain alive we will never give consent to subject ourselves to the dominion of the English.

For it is not glory, it is not riches, neither is it honours, but it is liberty alone that we fight and contend for, which no honest man will lose but with his life.'

The Abbey itself, founded in the twelfth century, is now carefully tended ruins. The Abbot's House has been restored as a museum. Arbroath is of interest insofar as it is a popular seaside holiday resort. Some of its past can be sampled down at the harbour where some old-style buildings are still used as gutting houses to produce the famous 'smokies': smoked haddock which are delicious. The Signal Tower Museum was originally built by Robert Stevenson, the lighthouse builder and grandfather of Robert Louis Stevenson.

The final stretch of this tour is southward, *via* the A92 into Dundee. A few places of interest can be taken in on the way. About a mile out of Arbroath, a turning to the right goes to Kellie Castle. Built in 1170, it was later restored in 1679. It is faced with pink sandstone quarried from nearby sources. The castle is very much lived in by the present owner who has made part of the building over into a Gallery of Scottish Artists, where artists and craftsmen can both exhibit and sell their work. A particularly attractive rose garden is worth seeing. Another right-hand turn opposite the Mains of Ardestie takes a minor

Monikie road (B962) to Monikie where, just west of the village, is Affleck Castle, dating from the fifteenth century. Over the years it has been kept in a fair state of preservation with the turreted keep the main architectural feature of this fortress of the Auchinlecks, hereditary armour-bearers to the Earls of Crawford. The B978 can now be joined at Monikie (instead of back-tracking to the A92) for the final run into Dundee.

Aberdeen

Tourist Information Centre
St Nicholas House, Broad Street, tel 23456

Population 190,200

Theatre
His Majesty's, Schoolhill

Cinemas
Capitol, Union Street
Grand Central, George Street
Odeon, Justice Mill Lane
Queens, Union Street
Cinema House, Skene Terrace
ABC, Shiprow

Places of Interest
Provost Skene's House, Flourmill Lane. Seventeenth century.

St Machar's Cathedral, Chanonry.

King's College. Fifteenth century.

Marischal College, Queen Street. Anthropological Museum.

Cruikshank Botanic Gardens. In Old Aberdeen.

Aberdeen Fish Market. An early rise needed to see the fish sales: 7.30.

Aberdeen Art Gallery and Museums, Schoolhill.

Aberdeen Maritime Museum, Shiprow. Provost Ross's House.

St Andrew's Episcopal Cathedral, King Street. The mother church of the Episcopal Communion in America.

Brig o' Balgownie. It stands $\frac{3}{4}$ mile north of High Street. Built in 1320 on the instructions of King Robert the Bruce, it is the oldest medieval bridge in Scotland.

Despite the fact that in recent years Aberdeen has become the 'offshore capital of Europe', the city has retained all the trappings of its long history and traditions. The 'oil industry' is out of sight: far to the east in the turbulent waters of the North Sea. Its presence in Aberdeen is only hinted at in the air of prosperity in the city's busy streets. The city has also held intact its long-standing association with the rural hinterland, acting as it has through the centuries as the social and commercial anchor which holds this north-eastern corner of Scotland together, so much so that the area has its own dialect of Scots which falls on the ear as a pleasant folk song. The motto of Aberdeen is 'Bon-Accord' (good fellowship) and the toast is the Toast of Bon-Accord: 'Happy to meet, sorry to part, happy to meet again'. Tied up with this is the welcome any visitor receives as a matter of course and inborn courtesy.

Aberdeen has been called 'The Granite City', from the white hard stone which gives its houses and buildings that sense of permanency and which exudes a sense of civic pride. Almost like the Royal Mile in Edinburgh, Union Street sums up much of Aberdeen's past. At its eastern end is Castle Street, known by Aberdonians as Castlegate. It is a square which has been the official centre of the city since the twelfth century. Despite the heavy traffic, this area still retains an echo of its long past. Here a crippled child once wandered about in the last decades of the eighteenth century who was to win a secure place in literature: George Gordon Byron, later Lord Byron. The focus of his attentions was a young girl, Mary Duff, who lived in No. 17 Castle Street, now the *Horseshoe Bar*, built around 1760. Many years later, when he had won European approval of his poetry, he wrote: 'Hearing of her marriage years after was like a thunderstroke'.

In the centre of the square is the Market Cross of Aberdeen, erected in 1686, which carries carved portrait medallions of ten Stuart kings beginning with James I of Scotland. Off Castle Street runs Shiprow, with Provost Ross's House, the second oldest remaining domestic dwelling, built in 1593. It is now fully restored and used as a maritime museum, celebrating Aberdeen's long history as a seaport. Almost as old is Provost Skene's House, tucked away in the courtyard of St Nicholas House, which now houses most of the city's administration departments. Dating back to 1545, it is also a period domestic museum and contains some remarkable exhibits. Among these is a cycle of religious paintings in tempera on the timber vault of the long gallery. These paintings were hidden under plaster for 300 years and are believed to date from 1622. In its time the House was used as the headquarters of the Duke of Cumberland on his way to meet Bonnie Prince Charlie's Highlanders at Culloden in April 1746.

On the east side of Broad Street is Marischal College with an elaborate neo-Gothic façade. A remarkable building, it was founded in 1593, to give Aberdeen its second university for a period of some 250 years during which England could boast only the same number! From Marischal College, down Upperkirkgate, one arrives at St Nicholas Church, dedicated to the patron saint of sailors, a fitting choice for a seaport. The church was first mentioned in a Papal Bull of 1157 and is worth a prolonged inspection.

Along the line of Schoolhill Viaduct there is the Central Public Library, St Mark's Church and His Majesty's Theatre, a trio of buildings once described as 'Education, Salvation and Damnation'. The Art Gallery in Schoolhill contains many examples from the Scottish school of painting, shown alongside French Impressionists, Post-Impressionists and the modern English School.

One could go on for a long time listing the visual delights of Aberdeen. What has been briefly described is merely the tip of the iceberg, for the city offers the visitor the chance to peep into a more than interesting past.

Travel services in the city are excellent whether by road, rail or air. The latter, centred on Dyce Airport, are now comprehensive since the coming of 'North Sea Oil'. Sea services connect Aberdeen with the Shetland Isles by the *St Clair*, a large comfortable ship which provides first-class accommodation with cars shipped on a roll-on/roll-off basis. From the bus station in Guild Street services cover the whole north-eastern area as far as Dundee, Inverness and Braemar.

There is everything and anything to do in Aberdeen, from basking on its beach, playing golf on the Queen's Links where golfing has been a town pleasure since 1625, to sampling the culinary skills provided in the many eating places, some of which offer a 'Taste of Scotland', and where advance booking is advised. At Hazlehead the city's public park offers a relaxing range of woodland walks, nature trails and golf courses, rivalled, perhaps, by Duthie Park.

Just as important, however, Aberdeen offers the visitor the chance to sample the hinterland of the Grampian Region, which is where our tour takes us.

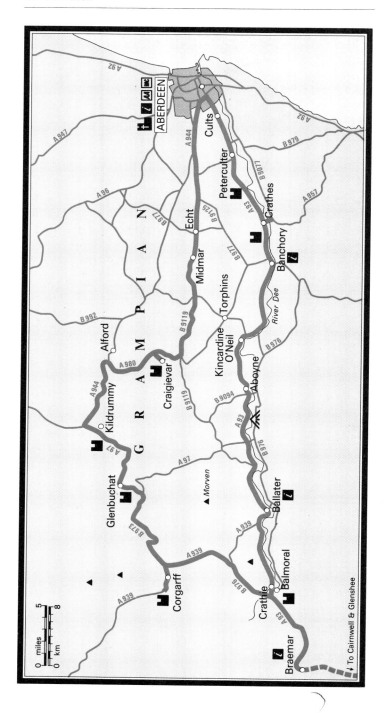

Aberdeen – Cults – Peterculter – Crathes – Banchory – Aboyne – Ballater – Braemar – Cairnwell/Glen Shee – Strathdon – Kildrummy – Alford – Craigievar – Midmar – Echt – Aberdeen

Tour length 140 miles

This tour takes the visitor from the high-technology world of the present into the past and into Royal Deeside. To Braemar, the road runs along the winding course of one of Aberdeen's two rivers: the Dee. The River Don is farther north and also touches our route. The route, too, is a transition from lowlands to highlands, with impressive scenic vistas which remain in the mind long after they are passed. Scottish vernacular in architecture is also seen in the castles along the route, ranging from the functional structure built to repel invaders, to the more relaxed times of last century when Queen Victoria and Prince Albert placed the Highlands firmly on the tourist map by the building of Balmoral, still a favourite residence of Britain's royal family.

Cults   The A93 runs south-west out from Aberdeen, through some of the city's suburbia, of which Cults forms a part. This is the western 'lung' of Aberdeen, where woodlands offer a daily escape for the city-dweller. West of Cults is Bieldside, closely connected with Blairs College, a seminary for the training of Roman Catholic priests. It has many treasures, including a Papal Bull issued by Pope Alexander III to the monastery at Ratisbon, once staffed by Scottish monks. Present-day Ratisbon is Regensburg in Bavaria, and is appropriately Aberdeen's 'twin city'.

Peterculter   The village of Peterculter (pronounced 'Petercooter') derives its name from an old chapel dedicated to St Peter, on the north side of the River Dee. The land on the south side of the river is known as Maryculter, from the chapel (now ruined) founded by the Knights Templar in 1187 on lands granted to them by King William the Lion of Scotland. Nearby is the mansion house of Kingcausie, part of which dates from the sixteenth century. It is said that Queen Victoria used to have her royal train to Balmoral stop here so that she could admire the facade of the house which is in the same style as that of Abbotsford, the Borders home of Sir Walter Scott. Peterculter owes its prosperity to the paper mills, founded in 1750, which produce high-quality paper for luxury publications. On from Peterculter is Drum Castle, where the original 1323 Charter, by which King Robert the Bruce gave the lands of Drum to William de Irwin, is on show in the castle's charter room. The view from the battlements is worth the climb!

Crathes   The sixteenth-century castle of Crathes is second only to Balmoral in its popularity with visitors. The building dates from 1553, when its construction began, and was completed 40 years later. In the words of the late Dr Douglas Simpson, an expert on Scotland's fortified houses: 'Externally this tower-house forms one of the most spectacular architectural conceptions in Scotland. Its regal coronet of round and square turrets, dormer windows with quaint finials and gargoyles of fantastic or grotesque design vie with the riotous exuberance of its ornate corbelling in forming a composition vibrant with élan and joy in life'. Prove that statement for yourself!

Banchory   Banchory is a 'modern' town dating from 1805, having grown from the original village of Arbeadie. Not only is it set in beautiful countryside, but it is also surrounded by history. Here St Ternan founded a monastery in the fifth century and traces remain of a medieval church. At Banchory Manse there is a Pictish wheeled cross. St Ternan's 'ronnecht', or Celtic handbell, can be seen at Inverey House, south of the town. A memorial tablet in the High Street commemorates the birthplace of James Scott Skinner, one of the best masters of Scots fiddle music and still unrivalled.

One of Banchory's industries is the Lavender Factory which welcomes visitors, as do most of the craft workshops in the area.

Kincardine O'Neil   The A93 runs westward through the oldest village on Deeside, Kincardine O'Neil, which has one main attraction: the thirteenth-century

ruins of the church of St Mary. The village of
Aboyne Aboyne derives its name from the Gaelic 'place of
rippling waters'. It is here that visitors come
from all over the world to see the Aboyne
Highland Games (in August). About 2 miles
north-west of Aboyne (on the B9094) is an
extraordinary collection of cairns, most of which
date from the Bronze Age. In the grounds of
Aboyne Castle is the Formaston Stone, a Pictish
sculptured cross slab with symbols and Ogham
characters, an early form of writing (short and
long lines cut across a horizontal datum).

Ballater The town of Ballater is really the creation of the
Victorian era. It was here that the Deeside
Railway ended – Queen Victoria insisted that the
line go no farther west, so as to preserve the
seclusion of her beloved Balmoral. And so the
track engineered to take the western end of the
line was converted into a simple lovers' walk. In
its time Ballater has seen many royal occasions,
all charged with the pomp and ceremony set
against the impressive backdrop of forest and
mountains, and 'Dark Lochnagar' reaching its
peak in the Forest of Balmoral. Nowadays visits
by members of the royal family are much more
informal, though still charged with excitement.
Among the attractions of Ballater is the
Monaltrie Park where rare and native animals
and birds can be seen.

The Mecca for most visitors to Royal Deeside is
Balmoral Balmoral Castle, open (May to July) six days a
week to the public, except when members of the
royal family are in residence. The castle is built
on a flat green shelf of meadow on the south bank
of the River Dee, with views southward through
the Forest of Balmoral to the long ridge of
Lochnagar with its eleven summits. The original
Castle of Balmoral dates back to 1484. Queen
Victoria's first visit to the area in 1848 was
followed by the purchase of the land by the
Prince Consort in 1852. The present castle was
re-built in 1855 in the Scottish Baronial style.

Braemar The most westerly point of this tour is Braemar.
Its castle dating from 1628, together with nearby
Invercauld Castle, has seen many of Scotland's
historical events and of its personages at its
door. Braemar is famous for the Highland Games

held in September and also for the Braemar Festival of music, drama and ballet. The Braemar Gathering is the climax of the Highland Games season in Scotland with some 60 athletic events – a far cry from its beginnings in 1817 when it started as a simple annual walk to raise funds for charity.

Cairnwell/ Glen Shee

Some 9 miles south of Braemar are the skiing facilities of the Cairnwell and Glen Shee which are being developed to rival those provided at Aviemore on the other side of the Grampian Mountains. Glen Shee takes the road south to the Spittal of Glenshee (a former shelter for travellers in the days when wolves roamed Scotland's wilder areas).

The return route involves re-tracing the road back to Crathie Church and taking the turn-off northward (B976) to Gairnshiel where the road joins the A939.

Strathdon

Strathdon, the upper parish of Donside, is a river valley which connects the five glens of the Deskry, the Nochty, the Carvie, the Ernan and the Comrie. Part of this road is a military road, constructed 200 years ago so that government troops could move quickly in the event of any trouble from Aberdeenshire's Highlanders. To the left of the junction between the A939 (known as the Lecht Road) and B973 is Corgarff Castle. This is a tower-house dating from the sixteenth century and later converted into a garrison post. Here in 1571 no fewer than 27 people fell victim to a blood feud between the Forbes clan and the Gordon clan, by being burnt to death.

Back along the B973, the route joins the main road (A97), a mile or so along which is Glenbuchat Castle. This was built in 1590 as the ancient seat of Clan Gordon on Upper Donside. It has a 'Castle Park' run by the Deeside Field Club. Over the castle entrance runs the motto: 'Nothing on earth remains but fame'. The last Laird of Glenbuchat was 68 when he actively supported the cause of Prince Charlie in 1745. For this he was hunted as a rebel and escaped to Norway; he died in poverty in Boulogne, France, four years later.

The road now hugs the north bank of the River Don for some 3 miles, when it strikes north and

Kildrummy enters the Den of Kildrummy and takes us to Kildrummy Castle. This thirteenth-century castle has seen much of Scotland's history enacted on its walls. It was captured in 1306 by Edward I of England, only one incident in its long and turbulent history. After the 'Forty-five' it was dismantled, but even in its present ruined state is able to impress and fire the imagination. In the Castle Gardens there is a Japanese water-garden. Close by Kildrummy is the old Kirk of Kildrummy, a medieval church with the fourteenth-century tomb of Forbes of Brux. On the way, at Glenkindie, are some examples of Pictish underground dwellings (a torch is needed to see inside the inner chamber of the best-preserved structure).

North of Kildrummy, our route now joins the Alford A944 eastward to Alford, through fine woodland. Alford is a market town with a population of some 1,300 and offers a number of attractions, including the Grampian Museum of Transport, with a display of transport used through the ages, from horse-drawn coaches to steam vehicles. Alford was the scene of a battle in 1645, won by the Duke of Montrose against the Covenanters; it was fought at the area between the village and the Don bridge in the failed cause of Charles I.

Southward on the A980 the visitor comes upon one of the most noble and notable of the Castles Craigievar of Mar: Craigievar, in which Scottish baronial architecture reached its greatest heights. Of the castle, it has been said: 'As a testimony of taste Craigievar ranks with any representative building in Britain. As a work of art it claims a Scottish place in the front rank of European architecture ... Quite perfect, lightly poised upon the ground, it is the apotheosis of its type'. The mingling of medieval and Renaissance features outside is also carried inside the castle by the many interior decorative delights, particularly richly moulded plaster ceilings. Perhaps one of the aspects of Craigievar's intimate feeling is that it is still a much-loved and lived-in home of the Sempills.

South of Craigievar, the route back to Aberdeen takes the minor road B9119 through typical rural

Midmar Aberdeenshire countryside. A stop at Midmar is more than worthwhile. Close by the church at Midmar is a stone circle, with a recumbent stone wedged between two huge pillar-stones or flankers. This circle, like many similar megalithic sites, dates from the Bronze Age in Scotland, proof that this fertile area of Scotland's north-east has been in continuous occupation by human population for many thousands of years. The fact that the circle of Midmar lies in the grounds of the seventeenth-century church is also evidence of millenia of continuous ritual, linking the distant past to the present. At Midmar there is a turreted castle dating from 1575 (no admittance).

Echt Another stone circle can be seen at Sunhoney Farm, about a mile west of Echt, one of a number in this particular area, and set among trees which lend their own atmosphere to the site. The Garlogie circle contains eight rough boulders within which are a number of small cairns. The site is supposed to be the tomb of a chief and of his dependants ritually killed at the time of his death.

The road soon joins the A944 into Aberdeen city. This 'Royal Deeside' route has many excellent restaurants, a number of which offer a 'Taste of Scotland'. These are found in Cults, Peterculter and Kildrummy. Good food, surely, adds flavour to any holiday.

Banff

Population 3,292

Places of Interest
Duff House. A magnificent example of Georgian baroque architecture
designed by William Adan in the 1730s. It contains an interpretative
museum.

St Mary's Churchyard. Only the sixteenth-century vaulted 'Banff Aisle'
remains.

Banff Castle. Built in 1750 on the site of a previous structure, some
parts of which can still be seen.

Collie Lodge. Built in 1836 in the form of a small Greek temple, it now
houses the Information Centre.

In its day Banff was a flourishing fishing port, with much of its
wealth being derived from herring. The end of this era came
when the harbour began to silt up and Banff had to look to
other means to maintain its economy. As the county town of
Banffshire, and a Royal Burgh since 1372, it has managed to
maintain a pleasant dignified atmosphere. The town is built on
three river terraces: High Street and Castle Street, Low Street
and Deveronside. These are connected by a series of steep,
narrow lanes which are sometimes stepped, giving this part of
Banff a medieval flavour (e.g. the Water Path). Some streets
have examples of seventeenth-century housing while others
present whole frontages of houses from the eighteenth century.
Banff was visited by Dr Samuel Johnston and his companion
James Boswell. Lord Byron's grandmother had a house on the
site of the present Court House. In front of the Town House the
Biggar Fountain marks the spot where in 1701 James
Macpherson, the Highland outlaw, was hanged. Firmly embedded in folk tradition, Macpherson played his fiddle before the
watching crowd and, when no one would offer to take the
instrument, he broke it. Then he went to his death. His defiance
is remembered in the song:

Sae rantinly, sae wantonly,
Sae dauntonly gaed he –
He played a tune and he danced it roun
Aneath the gallows-tree.

Much of the visual pleasure of Banff is due to the work of the

Banff Preservation Society, which has done sterling work in preventing the deterioration of the town's magnificent heritage in buildings. Banff was called the 'Bath of Scotland' in the eighteenth century when people went to coastal resorts to take advantage of the bracing sea air. It is an appropriate place to use as a base for a coastal tour. The landward side of the town, the fertile farmlands and hills of Banffshire and west Aberdeenshire, is just as enticing.

There is no railway, but bus services connect Banff to Elgin and Inverness westward and Fraserburgh, Peterhead and Aberdeen eastward, with other services to the villages in the Banff hinterland. Entertainment is provided in some hotels, with an emphasis on the traditional. The Duff House Royal Golf Club promotes an open competition during August which is becoming an important date in the national golfing calendar.

Banff – Macduff – Gardenstown – Pennan – New Aberdour – Rosehearty – Fraserburgh – Rathen – Peterhead – Boddam – Port Errol – Ellon – Pitmedden – Oldmeldrum – Huntly – Rothiemay – Fordyce – Portsoy – Whitehills – Banff

Tour length 115 miles

This tour combines the spectacular coastal scenery of the Moray Firth and North Sea with the more subdued farming countryside of Buchan and Banffshire. There are other contrasts, too. The small fishing villages strung along the Moray Firth, almost seeming to hang for dear life on cliff sides, may be compared with the rural settlements of long standing, some going back to pre-Christian times.

Macduff   Macduff is Banff's twin town. They lie on either side of the estuary of the River Deveron, linked by a road bridge dating from 1779, and with seven arches stepping purposefully over the Deveron's waters. Macduff dates from 1783 and is named after the Earl of Fife who owned the harbour in the former village of Doune. Now a busy bustling fishing port, the town is built on land that rises sharply from the shore. Despite its more recent dating, compared with Banff, Macduff has been successful in preserving no fewer than 123 'listed buildings' of architectural or historic interest, mainly among the fisher cottages in High Shore and Low Shore, at the eastern end of the harbour. One might catch sight of a large wooden anchor atop a rock above the harbour. This was retrieved in the nets of a local fishing boat and is supposed to date from the time of the invasion of England by the Spanish Armada in 1588.

There is much to do in Macduff. One can enjoy the facilities of one of the finest outdoor swimming pools in Scotland, or sample the cliff-top Royal Golf Course. A climb up to the summit of

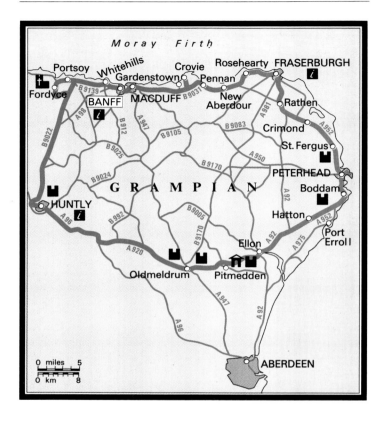

Doune Hill offers an excellent vantage point for some fine coastal views.

The A98 running eastward out of Macduff is now followed until the junction with the B9031. This is a road which offers some spectacular sights of the sea coast. Land hereabouts rises sheer from the sea, rather than in easy stages. Waves of grassy, green hills are pierced by deep-cut glens, each with its own stream. Three headlands dominate: Gamrie Head, Troup Head and Penan Head.

Gardenstown and Crovie The villages of Gardenstown and Crovie are 'musts' to see. The latter is an ancient cliff-foot village, in which the houses stand two-deep in a long line under the dominating cliff face. A footpath connection between the village and Gardenstown was washed away after a great storm in 1953 and fears were expressed for the possible desertion of Crovie. But the damage has since been repaired and Crovie still lives. Gardenstown was founded as a fishing village in 1720 and has managed to retain this role despite the economic problems in the present-day fishing industry. The houses of Gardenstown rise in tiers from the foot of the red-coloured cliffs. On the slope of Gamrie Mhor, to the west of the town, are ruins of an eleventh-century church, said to have been built in 1004 by the Thane of Buchan in fulfilment of a vow to erect a church if St John the Evangelist would help to defeat an invasion of Danes. The invasion was well met; three Danish kings died in the fighting, and St John had his church.

Pennan Picking up the B9031 again, the village of Pennan is found surrounded by cliffs in a small horse-shoe bay which was once a popular landing place for smugglers loaded with wines, silks and luxuries from the Continent. The village consists of one row of traditional fisher dwellings.

New Aberdour Pennan's neighbour, New Aberdour, a planned village dating from 1798, is close to a popular beach, flanked by rocky headlands, with many sea caves suitable for safe exploration by families. Old Aberdour Church is one of the oldest in the north of Scotland.

Rosehearty The village of Rosehearty marks the change of scenery from the low-lying sandy areas of the

Banff and Buchan coast to the more rocky cliffs that are a feature of the western parts of the Moray coast. Rosehearty is a holiday village and a dormitory suburb for Fraserburgh, 2 miles away. To the south of the village is the ruin of Pitsligo Castle, the oldest part of which dates from 1424. Both old and new kirks of Pitsligo can be seen on the road above the castle. The newer building incorporates some fine examples of Jacobean wood carving, transferred from the old kirk.

Fraserburgh The coast road from Rosehearty rolls into one of the major centres of population and industry in the Grampian Region: Fraserburgh. It was founded in 1546 as a fishing port and still serves the fleet which is based on the rich North Sea fishing grounds. The wide curve of Fraserburgh beach, backed by rolling dunes and stretching for some 3 miles to Cairnbulg Point, makes the town a popular tourist attraction, reinforced by many recreational facilities. The staff at the Information Centre (3 Saltoun Square) are more than helpful. On Kinnaird's Head north of the town is a lighthouse and the remains of the sixteenth-century castle built to guard the embryo town. Near this is the 'Wine Tower', a fifteenth-century three-storey building whose purpose remains a mystery, despite its name. The Broadsea area of the town is worth a visit, to see old-world buildings with red-tiled roofs. It was here that Marchese Marconi, the radio pioneer, had a research station from which signals were sent to receiving stations in England. Marconi Road reminds us of this connection.

The road (A92) southward out of Fraserburgh now takes us away from the coast into farmlands. **Rathen** At Rathen is the churchyard where lie the Scottish ancestors of the Norwegian national composer, Edvard Grieg. After Rathen, we pick up the A952 which runs into the parish of Crimond, which gives its name to the psalm tune to which the metrical version of the 23rd Psalm is **St Fergus** sung. St Fergus is typical of a small village being affected by North Sea development: it is now the place where the natural gas pipelines from the Brent and Ninian Fields make landfall.

Just where the road crosses the River Ugie, on

the outskirts of Peterhead, are the castles of Ravenscraig and Inverugie. Both are now in ruins. Inverugie Castle was the birthplace of Field Marshal James Keith, who won fame and fortune on the battlefields of Europe. Peterhead is entered on its north side.

Peterhead Peterhead is a major port for the white fish industry and is also a major on-shore terminal for the North Sea oil industry. Little wonder, then, that it has that kind of 'boom-town' bustle which, fortunately, has not detracted from the town's original function, dating from 1593, to be an important centre for sea and land-based commerce. The town once had a reputation for the curing properties of its water. One rather attractive feature of Peterhead is the extensive use made of the local red-tinged granite. Its massive harbour (begun in 1868) was finally finished in 1948 with the help of convict labour from the prison which lies to the south of the town. As one might expect in a town with a population of over 16,000, there are many facilities for visitors. Strangely, there is no manned information centre (there is an Information Point at the Links Car Park) though the staff at the Community Centre (Queen Street) are helpful.

There is a pre-Reformation Church, overlooking Peterhead Bay to the south of the town, dating from the twelfth century and worth a visit. The town's major attraction is, however, the harbour, where an astonishing variety of craft move constantly in and out between the interlinked basins of the 'National Harbour of Refuge', and where the visitor can absorb some of the realistic atmosphere when the fishing catch is bought and sold. For the background to the history of fishing in Peterhead, one must visit Arbuthnot Museum and Art Gallery.

The road south out from Peterhead is the A952 which, with other roads, will take the visitor gradually away from the Buchan coast and inland to quite different scenic vistas. A turn-off to the left at the village of Stirling will arrive at Boddam Boddam and Buchan-ness lighthouse. One of the most spectacular of its kind in the north, it was built in 1827 after a period of four years during which no fewer than 23 ship wrecks occurred. In those days there was a rule that no salvage could be claimed if anything living remained on a wreck, which gave rise to the malicious rhyme:

The Anna it came round the coast
And all the hands on it were lost;
Except the monkey that climbed the post
And the Boddamers hanged the monkey, O!

From the lantern balcony there is a magnificent view north and south and, indeed, inland, which should not be missed on any account, more so if the weather is clear. The massive construction works at Boddam is a new power station.

Port Errol   At Colwells, we now take the A975 into Port Errol. This little fishing village with its picturesque harbour is yet another of these eighteenth-century 'planned' settlements, now designated a conservation area. To the north of the village is Slains Castle, now in ruins, though it was sufficiently palatial to entertain Dr Samuel Johnson and his friend Boswell in 1773 when they used the castle as their base for a visit to the Bullers of Buchan. The Bullers are to the north of the castle and are in fact cliffs surrounding a 200-feet-deep cauldron carved by the relentless action of the North Sea. This is an awe-inspiring sight, with thousands of seabirds punctuating the air. It cannot be stressed too greatly that caution must be exercised if the Bullers are visited, because the cliff-top pathways are narrow and potentially dangerous. Slains Castle is supposed to have been the inspiration for the original 'Count Dracula' novel by Bram Stoker, who visited Slains for a holiday rest. The sands at Cruden Bay make this diversion from our main route rather inviting.

There are now two or three small side roads which can be taken to rejoin the A952. The **Hatton**   village of Hatton bases its prosperity on a bakery, employing over 200, which makes delicious biscuits. It was founded some 80 years ago by Forbes Simmers when he moved into Hatton with £60 and a borrowed horse: a typical case of Aberdeenshire enterprise.

At Old Birness the A92 and the A952 join forces **Ellon**   to run into Ellon, a large burgh still growing in its role as a commuter satellite of Aberdeen, though it retains its function as a market town. There is much new building here, though fortunately the planners have succeeded in retaining certain vistas, as witness the area on the banks of the River Ythan where once stood the old Castle of Ardgith, now only a fragment.

The A920 does a bit of contortion with the B999, just before it reaches the small village of Pitmedden. Signposting, however, allows the visitor to find his way easily. Just west of Pitmedden lies Udny Castle and, on the north side of the road, Pitmedden House with its Great Garden, one of the showplaces maintained by the National Trust for Scotland. Udny Castle goes back to the seventeenth century when it was finally completed. It has a stout rectangular tower crowned by battlements under a sloping roof and has angle turrets at each of the four corners. The green fields in this area were once full of stones, which were cleared completely to create good farming land and have been described as 'a monument to industry comparable only to the slave-built pyramids of Egypt'.

Joining the A920 once more the road goes into the quaint little burgh of Oldmeldrum, with some glorious views of the rise of Bennachie to the west and Mounie Castle 3 miles to the northwest. Barra Castle bears the dates 1614 and 1618 and is a massive tower-house with a new wing built in 1755. Mounie dates from 1590 and contains mementoes of Mary, Queen of Scots. It lies on the A920 route out of Oldmeldrum, which route takes the visitor through some pleasant wood and farmlands. At Colpy the road joins the main A96 into Huntly.

Huntly is a 'new town' of the eighteenth century and lies in the heart of the area known locally as Strathbogie. The town lies between two rivers, the Bogie and the Deveron, and has many buildings of architectural interest. The local Information Centre (in The Square) offers an architectural trail for those who wish to add a dimension of interest to a stroll round this neat town. Huntly's main attraction is the ruins of Huntly Castle: down Castle Street and through a long wooded drive. It started as a Norman stronghold built on a motte and was later

Pitmedden

Oldmeldrum

Huntly

extended in 1449. The end of the castle came in 1594 when it was blown up, but it was afterwards restored, a task which went for nothing when the owner lost his head after declaring support for King Charles I and the castle was left to fall into ruin. It still impresses the mind, however, and is worth an extended visit.

The road to be taken out of Huntly (B9022) goes north to the Moray Firth coast, on the final stage of this route. This is another pleasant leisurely drive during which one can take in much of the surrounding countryside. The little village of Rothiemay seems to sum up the easy-going pace of this run. The village lies on the banks of the River Deveron in the heart of the Deveron valley and affords some magnificent views. It is a pleasant place to rest for a while.

Immediately after Canterbury at the junction of the B9022 and B9023 take the left-hand turn (with a further right turn) to Fordyce, dominated by Durn Hill with its prehistoric fort. This is an old-world village, now designated a conservation area. It has an interesting history and has a charm of its own. The Church of Fordyce was first mentioned in 1272. It stood where the ruins in the old kirkyard still stand today. The tall belfry dates from 1661. Fordyce Castle stands in the middle of the village and was built in 1592, a model example of sixteenth-century Scottish Baronial architecture. Until 1964 Fordyce Academy, founded early in the eighteenth century by a son of the parish, was well-known in the world of education for its high standards which laid the foundations of the careers of many famous people, one of whom became a personal doctor to Queen Victoria.

The final port of call on this route before we return to Banff is Portsoy. Set alongside a wide sheltered bay, Portsoy was created a Burgh of Barony in 1550 and grew around the old commercial harbour, built in 1693. Once a major port for the herring fishery industry, the harbour now caters mostly for small pleasure craft. Many of the older buildings in Portsoy are now being restored and the town presents many delights to the eye with interesting wynds and closes to investigate: a real photographer's delight.

In the Portsoy district are to be found deposits of serpentine marble which has a subtle green and red colouring. Many jewellery souvenirs are made from this material; it was used in the finishing of the Palace of Versailles. The Marble Workshop and Pottery welcomes visitors (it is beside the harbour).

Whitehills The coast road to Banff passes the small fishing village of Whitehills, with its houses built right on the shore edge, their gable ends fronting on to the Moray Firth. It is one of the few fishing ports that have retained their independence, and many of the local fishing boats prefer it to the facilities offered at Macduff.

A short run takes us back to Banff.

The Bullers of Buchan

Elgin

Tourist Information Centre
17 High Street, tel 3388

Population 18,905

Places of Interest

Elgin Cathedral. Now in ruins, but still standing proud and magnificent, the cathedral dates from 1224. It has seen much of Scotland's history enacted in its environs. In 1390 it was burned by Alexander, Earl of Buchan, known as the 'Wolf of Badenoch'. In 1568 the lead was stripped from the roof to pay soldiers in the employ of Scotland's Regent Moray. The best preserved part is the Chapter House, dating from the early fifteenth century.

Cooper Park. The park is a public recreation ground with an attractive boating lake.

The Muckle Cross, Market Square. Erected in 1650.

St Gile's Church. In the middle of Elgin's High Street, this imposing building was erected in 1828 on the site of an older church.

Lady Hill. At the west end of High Street, this was the site of the medieval Elgin Castle, of which only a fragment remains. The tall monument at the top of the hill is that of the 5th and last Duke of Gordon. The castle is supposed to have been a residence of some of Scotland's early kings.

Near Elgin:

Findhorn. At the mouth of Findhorn Bay 12 miles distant, the site of a remarkable community whose work for peace has earned a growing world-wide recognition.

Burghead. A large fishing village with both Norse and Iron Age forts.

Spynie Palace. Two miles north of Elgin. Once the official residence of the Bishops of Moray. Now in ruins, but still impressive.

Lossiemouth. A coastal fishing village with a fine beach. Ramsay MacDonald (the first British Labour Prime Minister) was born here; his house may be visited.

Pluscarden Priory. Six miles south-west of Elgin. Founded in 1230 the priory was used until 1560, when it fell into ruins. In 1948 monks of the Benedictine Order (from Prinknash Abbey in Gloucester) returned and started a long-term programme of restoration. Well worth a visit.

Duffus Castle. A ruined fourteenth-century structure.

Elgin is an excellent base for touring the surrounding district of Moray, which offers not only marvellous scenic variety, but also sites of historic interest; in addition there is access to Scotland's whisky-distilling area and the ski-based resort of Aviemore. Acting, as it does, as a market town for the extensive farmlands around it, Elgin offers many facilities and attractions for the visitor, not least the mild climate of the Moray Firth with its low rainfall.

Elgin is on the main Inverness–Aberdeen rail route and is served by a regular and frequent rail service. The station is on the southern outskirts of the city (east of the junction of Moss Street and New Elgin Road). A full and comprehensive bus service links Elgin with all the major towns within a 50-mile radius or so. The bus station is on the north side, down Lossie Wynd which is just off High Street. There is a cinema, and Elgin Town Hall is frequently used for concerts and theatre productions.

Elgin can justly claim to be a city, though its cathedral is now in ruins. It has been for centuries a focal point for much of the history of the surrounding district of Moray which has also featured in the pages of Scotland's turbulent past. There is an air of justified quiet pride among Elgin's townspeople as they crowd the High Street. It is on this street that over a dozen historic houses of great charm can be seen. No. 7, Braco's Banking House, is a three-storey house with typical Scottish crow-stepped gables and dates from 1694. A number of these old houses have been restored (Nos 15–19, 21–25, 30–32). The small streets running off High Street are worth investigating, for they all reveal something of Elgin's past and are typical architectural examples of a Scottish seventeenth-century town boasting commercial wealth and civic pride.

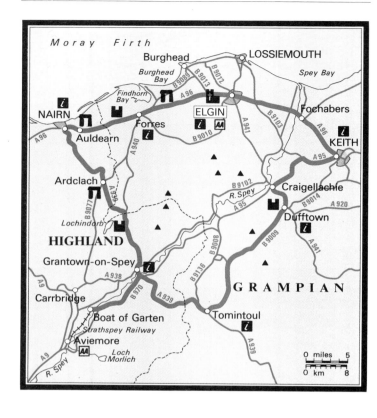

Elgin – Fochabers – Keith – Craigellachie – Dufftown – Tomintoul – Grantown-on-Spey – (Aviemore) – Ardclach – Nairn – Auldearn – Forres – Elgin

Tour length 110 miles; with Aviemore 140 miles

This tour runs through the fertile and wooded coastal plains of the 'Laich o Moray', and then into the sparse moorland of the foothills of the Grampian Mountains, through some of the 'Whisky Country' of the straths of the River Spey. This is largely a scenic tour, well provided with pleasant stopping off places with vantage points – to say nothing of the chance to visit one or two of the whisky distilleries and taste the 'wine of the country'.

The A96 major road runs east through the parish of Urquhart and Lhanbryde, once a sleepy hamlet but now a dormitory suburb of Elgin. Fochabers dates from 1776 when the 4th Duke of Gordon decided to plan a new town. Most of the buildings in the High Street are 'protected', which means that their owners cannot change their property if the changes detract from the original 200-year-old architectural concepts. Two major commercial attractions are based in the town: Christie's Nurseries and Baxter's Foods, the former dating from 1820 and the latter now grown into a household word for food products of the highest quality with a Highland flavour. Both these establishments are open to visitors, with guided tours offered at Baxters.

Gordon Castle (not open to the public) lies to the north of Fochabers. Founded in 1498, the castle was rebuilt totally towards the end of the eighteenth century. Holly trees in the extensive gardens are those in the original song *The Blue Bells of Scotland*, with the 'Highland Laddie' of the song being the Marquis of Huntly who accompanied Sir Richard Abercrombie to Holland in 1799 as Colonel of the 92nd Gordon Highlanders:

Oh, where, tell me where, is your Highland laddie gone?

He's gone with streaming banners, where noble deeds
are done,
And my sad heart will tremble till he comes safely
home.
Ah, where, tell me where, did your Highland laddie
stay?
He dwelt beneath the holly trees, beside the rapid Spey,
And mony a blessing followed him the day he went
away.

Continuing on the A96 for some 8 miles,
through the Forest of Speymouth, the road enters
Keith, on the River Isla and set among rounded
hills. The town was originally three separate
villages which merged into each other as they
grew. As we approach Keith from the north-west
a vast line of bonded stores indicates that we are
coming into whisky country. One-and-a-half million gallons of whisky are stored here, a kind of
Scottish Fort Knox holding liquid gold! Keith
itself has four distilleries. The eighteenth-
century 'Strathisla' distillery offers conducted
tours as do others on our route (part of the
'Whisky Trail').

In Holy Trinity Episcopal Church is the
'Seabury Chair' on which Bishop Kilgour sat
when he consecrated Bishop Seabury as the first
Bishop of the American Episcopal Church in
1829. Keith is also the birthplace of St John
Ogilvie, Scotland's first post-Reformation saint,
canonised in October 1976. A new Art Gallery,
housing a selection of high-quality modern
prints, is combined with the Information Centre.

We leave Keith by re-tracing the A96 for a mile
or so to pick up the A95 going south. This road
runs through the parish of Boharm and the
village of Mulben and the quaintly named
Maggieknockater to Craigellachie, where the
River Fiddich joins the River Spey, and where
four roads meet. The visual highlight is the
massive but elegantly designed iron bridge which
spans the Spey. It was built by Thomas Telford,
one of Britain's major engineers of last century,
and completed in 1815. It is a prefabricated
structure with the parts cast hundreds of miles
away at Plas Kynaston in Wales and then
brought piece by piece to the Highlands. A pair
of battlemented towers anchor the bridge from

Keith

Craigellachie

the right bank of the river to the base of the rock called Craigellachie. A new road bridge has been built to cope with modern traffic conditions, making Telford's magnificent single-span creation redundant, yet still something to view with some pleasure.

Dufftown   Our road now is the A941, through 4 miles of hill scenery to Dufftown, the real capital of malt whisky distilling, as noted in the couplet:

Rome was built on seven hills,
Dufftown on its seven stills.

Just before the entrance to Dufftown is the massive Balvenie Castle, a ruined thirteenth-century, originally moated, stronghold of the Comyns. It was visited by Edward I of England, the 'Hammer of the Scots', in 1304, and by Mary, Queen of Scots in 1562.

Dufftown was founded in 1817 by James Duff, 4th Earl of Fife, and named after him. The town was the birthplace (1829) of the Canadian statesman Lord Mount Stephen, President of the Bank of Montreal. At the south end of the town is Mortlach parish church, next to Mortlach Distillery (founded in 1823). The church dates from the twelfth century but there is evidence to suggest that there was a building here before that. In the year 1010, Malcolm II, King of Scots, won a battle over the Danes, and, as an expression of his gratitude, he added 'three spears' length' to the older church.

Both the Balvenie and Glenfiddich distilleries welcome visitors; the latter is on the 'Whisky Trail'. The golf course is reputed to have one hole at a greater altitude than any other in Britain above the 1,000-feet contour.

The route now is southward, taking the B9009 through typical Highland scenery and through Glen Rinnes and Glen Livet. On the right are the heights of Little and Meikle Conval. The latter was used, in the old whisky smuggling days of early last century, for lighting fires to warn the illegal distillers in Glen Rinnes that excisemen were on their way. At Lynemore a stone can be seen marked 'V.R. 24th Sept 1867'. This marks the spot where Queen Victoria stopped for a picnic before travelling on to Glenfiddich Lodge.

At Auchbreck, the road turns left to pick up the B9008 through Glen Livet. If one wishes to sample the product of the Glenlivet Distillery, one turns right for a mile or so. The distillery was founded in 1824 by George Smith, on whose efforts to legalise distilling the whole of the present whisky industry is based.

Tomintoul Continuing southwards on the B9008 we reach the village of Tomintoul, founded about 200 years ago. It is the highest village in the Grampian Region at 1,200 feet above sea level. Set between the River Avon and the Conglass Water, its bracing air makes it a popular holiday resort. The Visitor Centre in the Square has a re-constructed rural kitchen and a number of displays related to the town and its environs. Despite its population of only just over 300, Tomintoul offers an impressive range of tourist facilities. Were one not on a tour, one would really be tempted to 'rest one's caravan'. For instance, a few short walks provide some fantastic views of the Grampian Mountains and Glen Avon, one of the few unspoilt glens in Scotland.

Leaving Tomintoul on the A939, the road goes west through remote moorland with the Hills of Cromdale dominating the northern skyline. This road is built on one of the old military roads constructed to open up the Grampian Highlands so that the 'rebellious Highlanders' could be kept under control. With a little imagination one can imagine red-coated soldiers trudging their way from Tomintoul to Grantown-on-Spey, our desti-nation. Just before the A939 meets the A95 there is a cairn on the right-hand side of the road, one of many dotted around the countryside though most are off the beaten track.

Grantown-on-
Spey Grantown-on-Spey is yet another 'planned' town of the eighteenth century, this time found-ed by the Laird of Grant in an effort to establish a new economic focal point for the fertile area in which the town stands. The town is a planning delight. In particular, the Square is a town centre which is almost without equal in the Highlands, with trees almost 100 years old and beautifully belying their age. At the north-west corner of the Square is an eighteenth-century house with double windows, a reminder of the

days when house-owners had to pay a 'window-tax'. Just north of the town is Castle Grant (no admittance), parts of which date from the twelfth century. One of the towers is reputed to be haunted by the ghost of Lady Barbara Grant, who was walled up alive for her misdeeds. When Queen Victoria paid a visit to the castle she described it as 'a very plain-looking house, like a factory'. Robert Burns was once a guest at the castle, where he met the 'Bonnie Lesley' whom he later immortalised in song.

If time allows, a visit to Aviemore is recommended, which will add about 30 miles (15 miles each way back to Grantown) to the route length, but with an interesting diversion to enable one to leave the car for a while. The A95 goes south **Boat of Garten** through Dulnain Bridge to Boat of Garten. At the station here one can take a ride in one of the steam trains run by the Strathspey Railway Company between Boat of Garten and Aviemore (20-minute run). This branch line was closed in 1965 and rescued four years later by much hard work from willing volunteers to provide visitors with an interesting visual and physical contact with the past.

Aviemore   Aviemore is a thriving tourist centre based on the recreational activities offered by the Cairngorm range of mountains. The range of diversions is quite bewildering and the visitor will have to take a considered choice of what is offered. The Information Desk at the Aviemore Centre will provide details of the current activities in the area, which include nature trails, pony-trekking, sailing, canoeing, skating, skiing, swimming, bird-watching, golf and looking at the only herd of reindeer in Britain (at Glenmore). To return to Boat of Garten, take the steam train from the special platform behind the main British Rail station.

From Grantown-on-Spey the northward route is the A939 to Nairn on the shores of the Moray Firth. Take time to stop at the old parish church **Ardclach** of Ardclach, on the left bank of a loop in the River Findhorn, and its associated bell-tower about $\frac{1}{2}$ mile away on a hill. The church was built in 1626, and because of its secluded position it was decided to build the bell-tower (1655), which also served as a look-out. Said to be the highest tower of its kind in Scotland, it is a compactly-built cube of two storeys with two gables. A monument beside the approach track remembers Donald Mitchell (b. 1782) who was Scotland's first missionary to India.

Nairn   The burgh of Nairn is a popular holiday resort, whose climate is one of the sunniest and driest in Britain. It has a remarkable stretch of coast with both sand and shingle beaches and a championship golf course among its tourist attractions. Since it was a centre of the herring fishing industry last century, the Fishertown Museum (in the Laing Hall on King Street) is justly devoted to that era in Nairn's history. Colonel James Grant was born here in 1827. In 1860–3 he accompanied the explorer Speke when searching for the sources of the River Nile.

About 8 miles to the west (at Ardersier) is Fort George, one of the most outstanding examples of Hanoverian military architecture, begun in 1748 and the last in a chain of three built in the Highlands (along with Fort William and Fort Augustus). To the south-west (B9090) are the castles of Cawdor and Kilravock, the former name being familiar, thanks to Shakespeare's *Macbeth*, to every schoolchild in the English-speaking world. Dating from 1372, with later additions, the castle and its gardens are well worth a visit. About 1½ miles west of Cawdor, Kilravock Castle has been occupied continuously since 1640 by the Rose family. It was at Kilravock that Prince Charlie was entertained by the laird, on the eve of the Battle of Culloden in 1746, while the Duke of Cumberland slept in his town house in Nairn. On the following day the Duke arrived at Kilravock and asked: 'I believe you have had my cousin here?'

Auldearn   Leaving Nairn on the A96, we reach in about 3 miles the small village of Auldearn, with its line of low cottages which preserve an old-world atmosphere. Here one can see the Boath Doocot or Dovecot which stands on a motte which is all that remains of the twelfth-century castle of Eren. The Doocot was built in the sixteenth century as a living larder where pigeons (or 'doos') were kept and fattened for their meat. On

this hill is where the Duke of Montrose raised his
standard in 1645, to rally his forces against the
army of the Covenanters. Montrose won the
subsequent battle with brilliant tactics. Three of
the defeated Covenanters are remembered by a
monument in the north porch of Auldearn
Church. A little past Auldearn to the left and
between the railway line and the road, is
Hardmuir, supposed to have been the 'blasted
heath' where Macbeth met the three witches. It
is called 'MacBeth's Hill' on the map.

Forres   Forres is an ancient town, with a Charter giving
it the status of a Royal Burgh dating from 1496.
Its main attraction is its many parklands and its
adherence to the outlines of the medieval town
plan which have remained virtually unaltered. In
the High Street the Market Cross is reminiscent
of the Scott Monument in Edinburgh. On Cluny
Hill the Nelson Monument dominates the town;
it was erected in 1805, the year after the Battle of
Trafalgar, and was the first national monument
raised to commemorate Nelson's victory. Many
old houses survive from the seventeenth and
eighteenth centuries, with the typical Scots
feature of crow-stepped gables (seen at the
western end of the High Street: Nos 160 and 164).
At the eastern end of the town, a few hundred
yards along the road to Findhorn, is a remarkable sculptured stone, the largest in
Scotland, 23 feet high. The carvings tell the story
of a battle supposed to have taken place here
between the Scots and the Danes in which Seuno
(the stone is called Sueno's Stone), the father of
King Canute, took part. But the stone pre-dates
Sueno (better known as Svend Forkbeard of
Denmark) and is now reckoned to go back to the
ninth century.

The A96 offers now a straight and relaxing run
back to Elgin, with much to remember from what
is perhaps one of the most varied tours in this
book.

Inverness

Tourist Information Centre
23 Church Street, tel 34353

Population 39,736

Theatre
Eden Court, Bishop's Road

Cinema
La Scala, Academy Street

Places of Interest
The Town House, Castle Street. A Gothic-style building with many interesting features.

Museum and Art Gallery, Bridge Street. Devoted to the history of the Highlands with many tableaux. The Gallery is used for frequently changed exhibitions of pictures, sculptures and photographs.

Inverness Castle, Castle Street. Built in 1834 and now a court house.

Abertaff House, Church Street. Erected in 1592 and now the headquarters of the Highland Association devoted to the preservation of Gaelic and its culture.

Cromwell's Clock-Tower, off Shore Street. Erected about 1655, it is all that remains of the occupation of Inverness by the English forces of Oliver Cromwell.

St Andrew's Cathedral, Ardross Street. Built in 1869, it is richly decorated with illuminated windows and carved pillars. The baptismal font is a copy of the font in Copenhagen Cathedral.

Near Inverness:

Culloden Battlefield. Where the Highlanders of Bonnie Prince Charlie met the army of the Duke of Cumberland with tragic outcome. There is a visitor centre run by the National Trust for Scotland. Six miles east of Inverness by the A9 and B9006.

Fort George. Barracks built in the eighteenth century as part of a chain of such military headquarters along with Fort William and Fort Augustus. Twelve miles from Inverness just past Ardersier.

Cawdor Castle. Home of the Thanes and Earls of Cawdor for over 600 years, and linked with Macbeth. Twelve miles from Inverness.

Clava Cairns. This atmospheric site dates from the Bronze Age. About 1 mile south of Culloden.

The Boar Stone. The stone dates from the eighth century and is an example of the sculptured stones executed during the time the Picts ruled over much of Scotland. It displays a carved boar and other mystic symbols. About $1\frac{1}{2}$ miles along Stratherrick Road.

Inverness is often called the 'Capital of the Highlands'. Certainly from the visitor's point of view the town is a major centre from which visits to many parts of the Highlands can begin. Travel services are comprehensive. There are good railway links with Aberdeen ($2\frac{1}{2}$ hours), Glasgow and Edinburgh (4 hours). Dalcross Airport (about 8 miles east of the town) offers flights to Aberdeen, Glasgow and Edinburgh; to the north to Wick, Orkney and Shetland, and to the west to Stornoway, Isle of Lewis. Buses (from Faraline Park) serve the town and its hinterland. In addition to the theatre and cinema a number of hotels offer Highland entertainment during the summer months. The Ice Rink is also popular with visitors.

Inverness is an ancient town, but little earlier than the sixteenth century remains. The town has been changed considerably over the past decade or so to meet the needs of modern living. Its saving feature, however, is the River Ness with its tree-filled islands, which has justly earned for Inverness the title 'Paris of the North'. Some parts of the town still echo the past, however, such as the little houses on Douglas Row. Church Street has some interesting old churches and graveyards. One of the latter (High Parish Church with a vaulted tower dating from the fourteenth century) was the scene of executions of Highlanders after Culloden in 1746. An 'Execution Stone' is said to show bullet marks.

Inverness is the northern terminus of the Caledonian Canal (completed in 1822) and there are facilities available for trips down the canal into Loch Ness (perhaps to catch sight of 'Nessie', a tourist 'asset' which seems to appear before the eyes of a favoured few).

As befits a town geared to cater for visitors, both resident and in transit to other areas of the Highlands, there are many good eating places in Inverness, including restaurants and hotels which are open to non-residents. Most of the major restaurants and the hotels have a table licence with a number of hotels offering excellent wine lists to accompany specialist dishes, such as the *Glenmhor Hotel*. The *Merlin Restaurant* (Union Street) offers both European and Chinese dishes – extremely good and at reasonable prices.

Inverness – Beauly – Kilmorack – Struy – Cannich – Drumnadrochit – Invermoriston – Fort Augustus – Foyers – Dores – Inverness

Tour length 90 miles

This tour takes the visitor through many scenic changes, from wooded farmland to typical Highland glens of outstanding beauty. The main item of interest, however, is that the route largely skirts both sides of Loch Ness. The loch is 24 miles long and over 1 mile wide. The maximum depth is reckoned to be about 750 feet. Stories of a water creature have been in Highland tradition for centuries, ever since St Columba (who brought Christianity from Ireland first to Iona and thereafter through the Highlands) fought a battle of minds with a monster of sorts and banished it into the waters of Loch Ness. This happened in the sixth century. Since then tradition tended to keep its local knowledge to itself until some fifty years ago, when the creature was sighted. Over the years people have not only seen 'something' but photographed it as well. Monster hunts nowadays use highly sophisticated electronic equipment, and certainly some of the results have been sufficient to create doubts in the minds of the most secptical. There is as yet no scientific proof of the existence of the creature, popularly called 'Nessie'.

Clachnaharry

Beauly

The A9 leads north out of Inverness, past the basin of the Caledonian Canal and the small village of Clachnaharry, where the citizens of Inverness once watched fearfully for raiding Highlanders. The road skirts the southern shore of the Beauly Firth, a land-locked piece of water, which dries out into mudflats at low tides and brings a variety of birds to feed. Continuing past the junction with the A831 (which we join later) the road takes the visitor to Beauly (French: *Beau lieu*). A pleasant country town, its main attraction is its spacious Square. At the north end of the Square are the ruins of a Priory founded in 1230 for monks of the Cistercian order. The Chapel was restored in 1909, after it had been used as a burying ground for the MacKenzies of Gairloch since 1470. In the Square is the monument to the Lovat Scouts

(1905), a Highland Regiment raised in 1900 to act as a countering force to the Boer Commandos in South Africa. In the past, the Square was used four times a year for large fairs, to which country folk flocked to buy and sell their produce and services. Nowadays it is busy with tourists.

Retracing the A9 back to just before Lovat Bridge (which spans the combined confluence from the rivers of three glens, Strathglass, Glen Strathfarrar and Glen Cannich) the route is now the A831. It follows the run of the River Beauly into woodlands with typical silver birch trees, many of the beautiful weeping variety. At

Kilmorack Kilmorack there is one of the many hydro-electric power stations (there is another at Aigas just down the road) that are found in the Highlands converting water power into electricity. Visitors are welcome to see round the stations. The fish passes at Kilmorack and Aigas are usually opened each morning to allow fish to travel up the Beauly river, particularly during the spawning season. A minor road turning on the left leads to Beaufort Castle (no admission) which is a nineteenth-century mansion and at present the seat of the Frasers of Lovat. The building is on the site of the original castle destroyed in 1746 after Culloden. It is a glorious, if ostentatious, example of the survival in the Highlands of the medieval castellated tradition. Nearby are the Falls of Kilmorack.

Struy At Struy Bridge the River Beauly becomes the River Glass. Here Erchless Castle is splendidly maintained. A tower-house on the L-plan, it was built about 1600 by John Chisholm. Nearby is Erchless Motehill, a densely-planted mound used as the burial place of the Chiefs of Clan Chisholm in the nineteenth century. It is supposed that the hill was a man-made mound to accommodate the type of wooden fortification common in the twelfth century before stone castles proved themselves better able to withstand attack.

The road now runs alongside Strathglass. Its wide green meadows are the product of glacial silt built up to form fertile land. At Glassburn there is an interesting well dedicated to St Ignatius which has some strange inscriptions. At

Cannich Cannich four Glens meet – Cannich, Strath Glass, Urquhart and Affric. Cannich itself is a small dull village of scattered houses. If time allows one would recommend taking the minor road up Glen Cannich for a few miles. The glen is one of the loveliest in Scotland, thickly wooded and with high mountains looming to offer a unique vista to the eye.

Returning to the village of Cannich, we pick up the A831 once more to head east through Glenurquhart. About 3 miles from Cannich is Corrimony (right-hand turn-off). Here local tradition has it that in 1797 the first sheep farm was established by men from the south of Scotland, the first of many such farms which were to spread over the Highlands and which led to the clearance of local populations from their homes. But the main feature of interest here is the chambered cairn or passage-grave surrounded by a stone circle. The precise dating of this megalithic monument is still in dispute but is in the region of 3000BC.

The road east winds through the farmed lands of Drumnadrochit Glen Urquhart to Drumnadrochit (Gaelic: the ridge of the bridge). The village is really a collection of farm townships living in communal rural harmony. The route is now southward on the A82, a mile or so along which, at Strone Point, stand the ruins of one of the major fortified structures in the Highlands, Urquhart Castle, which is also used as a vantage point for those who hope to catch a sight of 'Nessie'. The present structure was built in the thirteenth century on the site of an Iron Age fort. It was occupied by English forces in 1296 and finally captured by the Scots in 1308. The castle was then used until 1689, when it was blown up and left in ruins after the Jacobite Rising. In recent years the castle has been 'tidied up' to great effect and the visitor cannot fail to be impressed by one of the biggest stone castles in Scotland.

Behind *Drumnadrochit Hotel* there is a permanent 'Loch Ness Monster Exhibition' devoted to the history of the sightings of the creature over the last 50 years or so, with many photographs which pose a serious question as to the existence of 'Nessie'. The hotel itself was first opened as an inn some time before 1763, and was an important post for changing coach horses on the long haul from Fort William to Inverness.

In Highland glens 'tis far too oft observed
That man is chased away and game preserved.
Glen Urquhart is to me a lovlier glen –
Where deer and grouse have not supplanted men.

These lines were written by John Bright, the Quaker radical reformer, when staying at Drumnadrochit in 1856. Since his day the population of the glen has been halved by emigration.

Balbeg   Not far past Urquhart Castle, at Balbeg, is the memorial to John Cobb who was killed in September 1952 while attempting to break the world water-speed record in the jet-engined *Crusader*. Seemingly, when the craft was building up speed for the measured mile it struck some waves and broke into a thousand pieces. The Memorial cairn was erected by folk of Glenurquhart who greatly respected Cobb as a hero of speed as much as for his gentle qualities.

The A82 now runs south along the shores of Loch Ness and offers some magnificent views not only of the loch itself but the wooded slopes on the south side which will be on our return route Invermoriston to Inverness. Invermoriston is a small village situated at the end of Glen Moriston through which the road goes to the west coast. Con-Fort Augustus tinuing on the A82 Fort Augustus is reached, clustered round the southern end of Loch Ness. Here locks join the waters of Loch Oich to Loch Ness. The fort which gives the town its name is derived from the military structure built in 1742. It was attacked and captured by the Jacobites in 1746 who destroyed as much of it as they could. It was not until 1876 that the site of the fort was acquired by the Benedictines of the English Congregation and the building of St Benedict's Abbey was begun. It is a grand building with many architectural features to catch the eye. Apart from being a monastery, it is also a boys' school. Visitors are made most welcome. Some of the buildings of the old fort are incorporated in the Abbey. In the Hospice there is an interesting model of the old fort.

In the town centre there is a 'Great Glen

Exhibition', devoted to the geography and history of the district, including an inevitable section devoted to 'Nessie'. Just offshore, to the north of the town, is Cherry Island, with its crannog (a man-made site built on logs as a retreat from attackers), now lying under water but still visible. Kilchumein Churchyard, on the banks of the River Tarff, is on the site of the original monastic cell of St Cumein, a post-Columban missionary. Among the graves is that of John Anderson, made famous by Robert Burns in the song *John Anderson, my jo, John.*

The return route to Inverness takes the B862 up the southern side of Loch Ness and along one of the original roads (now modernised) built by General Wade in the eighteenth century. Wade was responsible for building many important roads in the Highlands and some are still passable by foot. Between 1725 and 1740 some 800 miles of roads were completed by his 'highwaymen' as he called his soldier-roadmakers. A famous couplet (said to have been written by Wade himself) runs: 'If you'd seen these roads before they were made, you'd lift up your hands and bless General Wade'.

Sparse traffic on this road offers some useful peace and quiet to contemplate the scenery of moorland and loch with occasional large tree plantations to offer some variety. The road climbs to over 1,160 feet to Whitebridge View Point, after which it forks. The turn to the right takes one back to Inverness. But the minor road (B852) runs along the southern shore of Loch Foyers Ness to Foyers and this is the route now described. Foyers came into historical prominence in 1896 when the first factory for producing aluminium in Britain went into production. Its electrical energy came from the Falls of Foyers, whose waters were harnessed to create the first commercial hydro-electric power scheme. The factory closed in 1967, and the waters of the area are now used to feed an underground hydro-electric power station about $\frac{1}{2}$ mile inland from the shores of Loch Ness.

The Falls of Foyers were once a famous sight. They were visited by Robert Burns who penned the lines:

Among the heathy hills and rugged woods
The foaming Foyers pours his mossy floods

Sadly the waters are now a mere trickle, but
still worth a visit, and they are easily accessible
from the roadside. Also at Foyers is Frank
Searle's Loch Ness Monster Information Bureau.

A little distance from Foyers is Boleskine
House, now the home of Jimmy Page, the pop
star of 'Led Zeppelin'. Boleskine House owes
some notoriety to the follower of the occult,
Aleister Crowley, who, earlier this century, made
such a name for himself as a follower and
practitioner of the black arts. He was popularly
Inverfarigaig known as 'The Beast'. At Inverfarigaig there is
the Farigaig Forest Centre, which illustrates the
development of the forest environment in the
Great Glen. Seedlings of the old Scots Pine,
which tree once covered much of the old
Caledonian Forest of the Highlands, can be
purchased as an unusual souvenir. The road now
continues to hug the shore of Loch Ness to
Dores Dores. This is an attractive little place, which
seems to be popular with Nessie, because it is in
this vicinity that many appearances of the
creature have been made. Dores was the
birthplace of Captain John MacKay, one of the
discoverers of Queensland in Australia, where
the town of MacKay was built in his memory.
About 2 miles out of Dores, and on the shore of
the Loch, is Aldourie Castle, a baronial mansion
of the late nineteenth century, which incorporates an earlier tower dating from the seventeenth century.

The road from Dores is once again the B862
which runs back into Inverness. But before going
into the town, a visit to the Holm Mills might be
of interest. Visitors are made most welcome to
see round the mill and witness the manufacture
of woollen goods in the Highlands. All the
processes involved are on display, from the wool
off the sheeps' backs to the finished product.

Dingwall

Population 4,815

Places of Interest

The Town House. Built in 1730.

General MacDonald Memorial. On Mitchell Hill just south of the town.

Cromartie Obelisk. In the car park.

Parish Church. A Georgian building dating from 1801.

Tolbooth Tower, High Street. Built in 1777.

The burgh of Dingwall is ideally placed for any visitor who wishes to sample a quite bewildering variety of scenery, to say nothing of a range of activities which would make any holiday memorable. Train services take one north and west (and south to connect with Inverness). Bus services offer both local runs and extended routes. And, as befits a well populated area, a comprehensive system of inter-linked roads provides easy access to many places of interest.

Dingwall owes its origin to the Norsemen who landed at the head of the Cromarty Firth to establish for themselves a centre of importance. The name Dingwall is derived from *Thing Vollr*: Council Place. It was created a royal burgh in 1226 and had its castle to stress its importance. The stones of the castle were incorporated in the eighteenth-century tolbooth tower in the High Street, and all that remains of the castle is a flanking tower at the foot of Castle Street. The whole flavour of Dingwall is that of an old-world rural market town. On the south side a tall square tower commemorates General Sir Hector MacDonald, the hero of the Battle of Omdurman, who rose from the ranks to become Governor of Ceylon. He died in Paris in 1903. Dingwall is the reputed birthplace of Macbeth, only one of the many interesting historical facts to be found in this area. In the Town House there is a museum devoted to local history, with a special exhibit devoted to the career of General MacDonald.

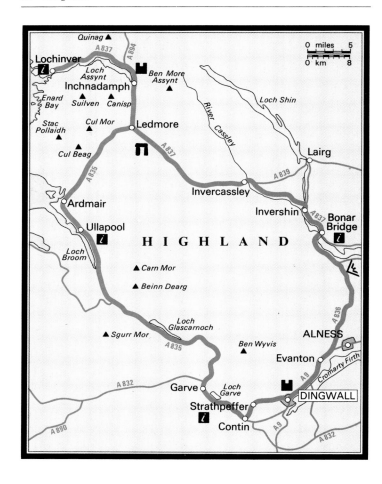

Dingwall – Strathpeffer – Contin – Garve – Ullapool – Ledmore – (Lochinver) – Invercassley – Invershin – Bonar Bridge – Alness – Evanton – Dingwall

Tour length 121 miles; with Lochinver 159 miles

The suggested route will present the visitor with many sharply-featured contrasts in scenery: from the fertile, low-lying hinterland around Dingwall to the rolling moorland and high spectacular mountains of the west coast of the Highlands; from densely-populated areas to remote communities located both inland and on the coast. If the mileage might seem rather high, particularly if the Lochinver visit is included, please be reminded that much of this mileage can be taken at a higher than average speed which will not in any way detract from the scenic beauty of the west. The mountains there reduce the human element to almost microscopic proportions. Indeed there are times when it seems as if no progress is being made, so impressive are these horizon-dominating heights.

Strathpeffer

The route out of Dingwall is the west-going A834, following the run of the River Peffery in a lush valley fringed by old poplar trees. About 5 miles on, the little village of Strathpeffer is reached. In the eighteenth century sulphur springs were discovered here and in no time at all Strathpeffer became a popular health resort, situated as it is in a natural amphitheatre of green hills under the looming mass of Ben Wyvis. The village has made an effort to restore the former railway station into a visitor centre and the result is delightful. There are craft workshops and an audio-visual display depicting the natural history of the Highlands. Strathpeffer itself is a pleasure to stroll around. Although the health-seeking Victorian and Edwardian crowds have long since disappeared, it does not require much imagination to envisage Strathpeffer in its heyday.

About a mile north of the village is Castle Leod (no admission), dating from 1606 but since rebuilt. It is the home of the Earl of Cromartie. One rather interesting walk (4 miles) is to

Knockfarril, a prominent ridge to the east of the village where one can see the remains of a vitrified fort (the stones have been fused together by great heat).

Contin   The A834 joins the A832 at Contin to strike westward towards beckoning mountains. Contin can be used as the base for a visit to the Rogie Falls where a suspension bridge strung out over the rapids makes a good vantage point to see leaping salmon in their seasonal runs up-river. Otherwise, continue along the A832 and stop the car at the picnic site close by the falls. At the western end of Loch Garve, mostly seen from the

Garve   roadside, is the village of Garve, a typical Highland community where peace seems to reign supreme. From Garve the road turns left to take the A835 through Strathgarve. The 20 miles to Braemore includes some spectacular scenery, with the height of Ben Wyvis dominating the scene on the right. One important road hazard to be watched for is deer crossing, particularly beside tree plantations. These animals are a common sight hereabouts. At Braemore Junction our route continues north to Ullapool, latterly running along the shores of Loch Broom. Corrieshalloch Gorge is a few hundred yards from Braemore Junction. This is a narrow cleft nearly 200 feet deep into which the water tumbles. The mile-long gorge is spanned by a fragile swing bridge.

Ullapool   Ullapool serves as the ferry terminal for the Island of Lewis. It is a striking sea town. Established as a port for the herring fishery in 1788, it still plays this role for the many fishing boats which ply out of Loch Broom. It is also a popular tourist resort and as such has much to offer the visitor, including a number of sea trips to, among others, the Summer Isles lying at the entrance to Loch Broom. Altogether Ullapool is a lively place with the sea at its doorstep. North from Ullapool is another straight run of some 18 miles passing through the small hamlets of Ardmair, Strathkanaird, Drumrunie, Knockan and Elphin, before reaching Ledmore. To the left of this run are the Coigach mountains and the heights of Inverpolly Forest, prominent among which are Cul Beag and Cul Mor, punctuating the sky with their impressive masses, with the strange-shaped needle-ridge of Stac Polly adding no little interest to an area dominated by mountains rising from insignificant foothills. This is wild country, vast and remote, where the presence of man takes second place to Nature.

Ledmore   A decision must now be taken at Ledmore. A visit to the port of Lochinver adds a round trip back to Ledmore of some 38 miles but it is a worthwhile excursion which will add a memorable dimension to this route. Let us take it then...

The road to Lochinver takes us again through some magnificent mountain scenery. Catching the eye on the left are Suilven (the Sugarloaf mountain) and Canisp, and on the right is the massif of Ben More Assynt. The confluence of the river Allt-nan-Uamh (River of the Caves) and the River Loanan makes an interesting stop. A short trek up the course of the river will take one to some caves in which prehistoric animal bones have been found, along with traces of occupation by early stone age man. The caves are at the base of a limestone cliff.

Inchnadamph   At the head of Loch Assynt is Inchnadamph, a fishing and climbing centre. From this little village, looking south, are new prospects of Suilven and Canisp and, to the north, the awe-inspiring Quinag and Glasven, which has the highest waterfall in Britain: a vertical drop of 658 feet, which is four times the height of Niagara. It requires, however, a good 3-mile walk from the road to reach this outstanding natural feature.

As the road skirts the head of Loch Assynt, the ruins of Ardvreck Castle can be seen. It was here that the Marquis of Montrose was captured in 1650 before being taken to execution in Edinburgh. The castle was once the stronghold of the Clan MacLeod of Assynt. The road now follows the winding River Inver through pleasantly wooded country into Lochinver.

Lochinver   Lochinver is one of the major fishing ports on the north-west coast of Scotland. It is a popular holiday spot for walkers and climbers, but its main attraction is as a centre for sea-angling and freshwater fishing, with access to over 300 lochs supporting brown trout. There is an interesting stone-craft workshop which can be visited to witness the craftsmen at work producing souvenirs. Now it is back on the road to Ledmore.

At Ledmore the A837 strikes eastward through wild country, as remote as one could ever wish for. Even so, there is evidence that prehistoric man found this area amenable as a place to live in. On the left hand side of the road bordering on Loch Borralan there are three sites of chambered cairns. If one might be surprised at this, it should be remembered that climatic conditions were quite different a few thousand years ago, and the environment was wooded and inhabited by wild boar, deer and other animals which were hunted for food. What one sees in the Highlands today represents the devastation by Nature and Man combined.

The road from Ledmore passes two more chambered cairns close by the junction to *Benmore Lodge Hotel.* We now pass through Strath Oykel to Oykel Bridge, beyond which there is a magnificent view of Ben More Assynt. A similar breathtaking mountain vista featuring the peaks of Cul Beag, Cul Mor, Suilven and Canisp is something to excite the eyes a little farther on.

Invercassley The settlement of Invercassley is a scatter of houses for forestry workers. The spot where the road crosses the River Cassley, at Tuiteam, was the scene of a bloody battle between the MacLeods of Lewis and the MacKays which took place in 1408. There is an ancient burial ground here. The MacKays won the day with only one MacLeod managing to escape back home to the Island of Lewis where he eventually died of his wounds. At Invershin the Rivers Cassley and Oykel start to feed their waters into the Kyle of Sutherland. Just beyond can be seen Carbisdale Castle, now a youth hostel.

Bonar Bridge The A837 ends at Bonar Bridge, a straggling village where the main route, the A9, runs both north and south. The southern route crosses a magnificent iron bridge spanning the entrance to the Dornoch Firth. In about 4 miles we take the fork to the right (A836). This road climbs up to the Struie Viewpoint. This is a marker on the left-hand side of the road from which one can identify the prominent landmarks in the area, including a superb view of the Dornoch Firth. The road then continues through high plateaux of hill and moorland before it descends through pleasantly wooded land to Alness. Along this route, to the left, one can catch a glimpse of the Cromarty Firth and Invergordon with its industrial sites such as the oil-platform building yard at Nigg and the aluminium smelter at Invergordon.

Alness   Although Alness looks 'new', because of the houses erected for the industrial population of the area, it is in fact a historic community with a long lineage. The A9 is joined once more at
Evanton Alness which takes us south through Evanton. This village lies at the foot of the Black Rock Ravine, which is an extraordinary cleft, some 2 miles long, through which the River Glass rushes to the Cromarty Forth. The A9 now runs along the shore of the Firth into Dingwall.

If this route has seemed somewhat long, there has surely been ample compensation in the ever-changing scenery from east to west and back again. If nothing else it has given the visitor the chance to sample the remoteness in which many small Highland communities exist, and which they accept willingly simply because of the special dimension to life and living which only mountains can offer.

Wick

Tourist Information Centre
Whitechapel Road, tel 2596

Population 7,933

Cinema
Pavilion, High Street

Places of Interest
The Harbour. Dates from 1810.

Carnegie Library and Museum.

Parish Church. The building dates from 1830 and the graveyard from 1576.

Caithness Glass Factory. Visitors are welcome to see glass blowing in progress.

Castle of Old Wick. A fragment dating from the twelfth century standing 1½ miles south of the town.

Much of the prosperity of Wick in the past was based on the herring fishing industry. Now the large harbour services the catches of white fish which are sent daily to markets in the south. The town's industries include a glass factory and a whisky distillery among others established in recent years.

The town's past dependence on herring is remembered in the displays in the Museum in the Carnegie Library (corner of Cliff Road and Sinclair Terrace) and in the recently opened Wick Heritage Centre. The older parts of Wick are worth strolling through, offering the visitor, as they do, the chance to pick up some of the atmosphere of the town's past days of glory when the herring was king. Wide streets, tree-lined squares and dark-stone built houses all lend their elements in a blend of charm.

Of equal interest, and a delight to the eye, are the products of the factory at Harrowhill, where glass jewellery and paper-weights are made, along with a range of other products. Visitors are welcome to see skilled workers producing works of art from molten glass.

The River Wick is a slow-moving river at the best of times, but still manages to give the town a piece of real estate which many other places would envy. It empties into the waters of Wick harbour, the beginnings of which date to 1808 when the British Fisheries Society commissioned engineer Thomas Telford to lay out a village on the south side of Wick, called Pultneytown. Later harbour improvements were engineered by the grandfather of Robert Louis Stevenson, the author of *Treasure Island*. If the hustle and bustle of Wick's harbours are memories of days long past, there is still plenty of activity to watch when local boats unload their catches of white fish caught in the Moray Firth and the North Sea.

Wick is serviced by rail (Inverness), bus and an airport (Inverness, Aberdeen, Orkney and Shetland).

Castle of Mey

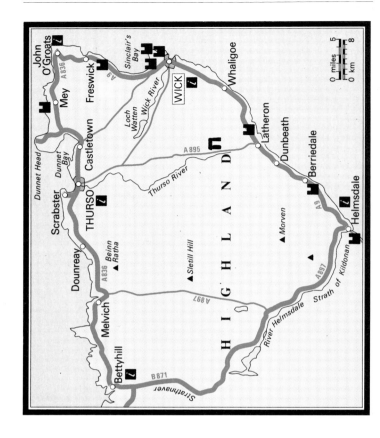

Wick – Keiss – Freswick – John o' Groats – Mey – Castletown – Thurso – Scrabster – Dounreay – Melvich – Bettyhill – Strathnaver – Strath of Kildonan – Helmsdale – Dunbeath – Latheron – Wick

Tour length 150 miles

This tour offers the visitor two main attractions. First, there are the varied seascapes along the north-eastern and northern coasts, the latter fronting the ever-turbulent Pentland Firth, and ranging from high cliffs rising sheer from the sea to low-lying flatlands with sand beaches. Second, there is the landward route which takes the visitor deep inland to traverse some of the glens (straths) which are today silent witnesses to the clearance of populations last century. Along the route lie many places of interest, all touching a history going back some 4,000 years. Some of the route is single-track road provided with ample passing places. Keep your eyes on the road ahead and use these passing places for other cars to overtake or to pass you from the oncoming direction.

Keiss The road north out of Wick, the A9, runs along the coast, first to Keiss where there can be seen the remains of the sixteenth-century castle close to its nineteenth-century successor. There are also in the vicinity what is left of two mesolithic brochs, proof that this area has attracted human habitation for over 2,000 years. Just south of **Freswick** Freswick is Bucholly Castle, which dates from the twelfth century, and was once the seat of Sweyn Asliefson, a Norse pirate who appears in the Orkneyinga Saga. In Freswick Bay the outline of a Norse settlement can be seen, now covered with blown sand since it was excavated in 1937. Sweyn's activities took him to Dublin, which he captured. Many other places in the British Isles received his attention on his looting and plundering raids.

John o' Groats John o' Groats is not quite the most northerly point on the British mainland as often claimed. That point is Dunnet Head, farther to the east. The name John o' Groats is derived from Jan de

Groot, one of several Dutch brothers who settled in Caithness in the reign of James IV of Scotland. With their subsequent prosperity came quarrels as to who had precedence at the family gatherings, which were resolved by John designing a house with eight walls, windows and doors, and an eight-sided table so that each claimant could imagine his own importance. From here there are views across the Pentland Firth to nearby offshore Stroma island and, farther away, Orkney. A short trip to Duncansby Head offers a view of the three stacks of Duncansby, natural rock pillars standing in the sea at the entrance to the Pentland Firth.

From John o' Groats the A836 goes westward to Thurso. Canisbay Church is fifteenth century, with additions from the seventeenth and eighteenth centuries. The outer south wall has a monument recording the death in 1568 of Donald Grot, son of John.

Mey   The castle of Mey (originally Barragil Castle) is now the home of Queen Elizabeth, the Queen Mother. Dating from 1586, it has been restored with much loving care. Though the castle is not open to the public, during the summer months the gardens are made available for the raising of funds for local charities. From the village of Dunnet, one can take the short road to Dunnet Head, a sandstone promontory from which some magnificent views fill the eye. It is supposed that this most northerly point in Scotland was first mentioned (as Cape Orcas) by Diodorus Siculus, the geographer of Julius Caesar (53 BC).

Castletown   The village of Castletown was built to house workers in nearby stone quarries, which produced Caithness flagstones used to pave the streets of cities throughout the world including Paris. Many of these flagstones can still be seen around Caithness, acting as walls or dykes to separate fields. The advent of concrete finished off an industry which in its day yielded some £30,000 per annum, a large sum in those days of the last century when a man was said to be 'passing rich' at £20 a year.

Although Wick is the 'county town' of Thurso Caithness, Thurso is the larger centre, with a population of over 9,000, derived mainly from the workforce at the Atomic Research Station at Dounreay. Like Wick, Thurso has its river. In its day, Thurso was a main port for shipping from northern Europe and Scandinavia, and was in its heyday when the flagstone industry was at its peak. Today it is mainly a market town and its rhythms are still largely those of the rural hinterland it serves. One of the oldest buildings in Thurso is St Peter's Church, erected in the thirteenth century and used until 1832 when the congregation moved to another venue for their services. The church is now being restored. The Folk Museum presents displays showing local life over the centuries. The library at the south end of Sinclair Street houses the fossil collection of Robert Dick, a local baker whose interest in botany and geology eventually made him a household name in scientific circles in Victorian times. Also on show are two early Christian stones, sculptured and incised with Scandinavian runes.

Scrabster   North-west out of Thurso (A836) is Scrabster. This is the harbour for the ferry which takes cars and passengers to Stromness in Orkney, and to the Faroe Islands. It is also a haven for fishing boats. The road now runs west to follow the coastline of the Pentland Firth. This is a treacherous stretch of water, notorious for its fast-flowing tides (6–10 knots). Its name is derived from 'Pictland', the Picts being a race of folk in Scotland ('the painted people') whose only remains are their many carved stones, and some elements of their language in place-names (for instance, Pitmedden in Aberdeenshire).

The road from the Scrabster turn-off runs through varied coastal scenery, with the sea on one side and, in the forward distance, the majestic rises of the mountains of western Sutherland. Eight miles from Thurso is Dounreay with its atomic reactors built in 1954 and now providing a significant amount of electricity. Whatever controversy might be raised about the use of nuclear power, there is no doubt that the shining steel sphere of Dounreay is a sign of the future in the present. And to explain the nature of atomic energy there is a permanent exhibition at Dounreay.

West of Dounreay, the road runs along the coast to the first of a string of interesting villages, many of which were established during the times of the Sutherland clearances. Melvich consists of a cluster of houses overlooking a bay into which the River Halladale flows, adding its fresh clear waters to those of the deep Pentland Firth. All along this coast there are sandy beaches and rocky outcrops which add their own particular character to the scenery. The village of Bettyhill was named after Elizabeth, 1st Countess of Sutherland. Situated at the mouth of the River Naver the village is a reminder of a tragic aspect of Highland history. To the east of Bettyhill is the former church of Farr, with a contemporary eighteenth-century pulpit and a Celtic cross. The church has been converted into a museum devoted to the theme of the clearances which took place in Strath Naver (1812–19) and the life style of the folk who lived through that period. Both Strathnaver and Kildonan (*see below*) saw large numbers of the population violently removed from their homes by the factors of the 1st Duke of Sutherland, so that the land could be given over to the grazing of sheep. For nearly half a century this removal process continued at such a scale that even such European figures as Napoleon and Karl Marx were moved to commit their thoughts to paper and condemn the system. An eyewitness of 1819 has described counting on one night the flames of 250 crofts, including his own, as homes were put to the torch. Many of those cleared either emigrated to the Americas or were re-settled on the infertile coastal lands of Sutherland and Caithness.

Melvich

Bettyhill

Strathnaver

The road now turns southward (A836) alongside the course of the River Naver. Peaceful though this route is, there were once many hamlets strung along the glen.

Strath of Kildonan

At Kinbrace the road (A897) goes through the Strath of Kildonan. This strath also suffered during the clearances, with some eighty per cent of its population being removed from their homes and crofts. Kildonan has, however, another claim to fame: nothing less than the 'gold fever' of 1867–69, which caught thousands of hopeful prospectors. The source of the gold was the

Suisgill and other burns in the area. It was even claimed that the teeth of grazing sheep were plated with gold, so plentiful was precious metal. The gold workings lasted for two years, with only a few making enough money from their panning to say that their efforts had been repaid. For hundreds of others it was personal disaster.

Helmsdale   Helmsdale is a small fishing village used by local fishing boats. The village was constructed by the Duke of Sutherland as a show-piece for some of his evicted tenants. The castle, now in ruins, overlooking the harbour was the scene (in 1567) of the poisoning of the Earl and Countess of Sutherland by a member of the Sutherland family who had ambitions for her son. Unfortunately, the son also inadvertently drank the fatal wine and he died. It is this incident which is thought to have inspired the poisoning scene in Shakespeare's *Hamlet*.

The road north to Wick again is the main A9 and takes the visitor through interesting coastal scenery and the inevitable facets of history. At Berriedale   Berriedale, where the road dips and rises in spectacular gradients, there are the tumbled ruins of a castle, once the fortress of the Earls of Caithness. After Berriedale Brae is climbed, using a sensible and well-advised low gear, a high cliff plateau is reached, to the left of which one can see the conical rise of Morvern, the only mountain of any respectable height in Caithness, with its neighbour, Scaraben, running an aspir-
Dunbeath   ing second. Dunbeath also has its castle, mostly dating from 1428 and still inhabited. The oldest part of the building is some two centuries earlier. The castle was besieged by Montrose in 1650 and captured after three days. Dunbeath is the birthplace of Highland novelist Neil M. Gunn, whose work has embodied so much of Highland history. His novel *The Silver Darlings* is set in Dunbeath in the days of the last century when the harbour was a busy herring port. It is now derelict. Two miles north of Dunbeath is the restored croft of Laidhay. Now a museum, the building dates from the early eighteenth century and shows a typical interior of the times.

Latheron   Latheron is another small coastal village, with its picturesque harbour (Latheronwheel) which once had no fewer than 35 fishing craft based here to support the prosperity derived from the herring, the 'silver darlings'. Latheron Parish Church is now a museum to Clan Gunn, a common surname in these parts, going back to Viking times. If one's interest is in the historic past of Caithness, then this is the area to see some impressive remains. Some 4 miles north-west of Lybster are the Chambered Tombs. One, the Round Cairn, is reckoned to be the finest tomb of its period on the Scottish mainland. The cairns date from the Neolithic/Bronze Age (2250–1750 BC).

Back on the A9 a visit to the 'Hill o Many Stanes' is worthwhile. Here, on a low hill, are 22 rows of small stones, with eight or more stones in each row. Experts have dated this structure to about 1800 BC, though the purpose of the unusual alignments is still unknown. A road sign on the A9 at Mid Clyth is easily seen for this rather unusual relic from 4,000 years ago. At Garrywhin ($6\frac{1}{2}$ miles south of Wick and about $\frac{1}{2}$ mile off the A9) there is a chambered tomb of the 'short-horned' type, typical of Caithness. It is known locally as the 'Cairn of Get'.

Just before one returns to Wick and the present: one last reminder of the past dependence of Caithness on the former herring industry at Whaligoe and Sarclet havens. At Whaligoe there are no fewer than 365 steps descending to the harbour. In the heyday of this curing station, herring in creels or baskets were taken up these steps, many times a day until the whole day's catch was unloaded. It needs little imagination to picture the hard work of a former generation which has resulted in the atmosphere of well-being that one finds in Caithness today.

Whaligoe

Kyle of Lochalsh

Tourist Information Centre
Information Centre, tel 4276

Population 803

Places of Interest
The village has little to offer of great interest but the following easily accessible places are worth a visit:

Eilean Donan Castle. See p.

Balmacara Estate. This includes the National Trust for Scotland Lochalsh Woodland Garden.

White Island. This was for a time the home of the late Gavin Maxwell, author of *Ring of Bright Water.*

Using the small west coast seaport of Kyle of Lochalsh as a base, the visitor is faced with a choice of tours. He can visit the Isle of Skye or choose the area of Wester Ross, which has such magnificent scenery that it is quite second to none in the British Isles. Of course, the matter is easily resolved if the visit to this area is for two or three days. On the basis that the time is in fact available, this chapter covers both Skye and Wester Ross. The extended stay will be well worth it.

Kyle of Lochalsh itself is a small but typical west coast of Scotland fishing port, whose main role, however, is to act as the car-ferry facility to Skye. In past years it was also the steamer port for the Western Isles, a role now filled by Ullapool farther north. As a holiday base it caters well for visitors. It is also the rail terminus for the train from Inverness, the 'West Highland Line', continually under threat of being axed by British Rail but managing to stay the execution because of its role as a popular route with tourists and its link with the many remote communities along its track. A local bus service is available, mostly used to link the communities on the Kyle peninsula.

Tour of Wester Ross

Kyle of Lochalsh – Balmacara – Eilean Donan – Stromeferry – Strathcarron – Achnasheen – Kinlochewe – Inverewe – Torridon – Shieldaig – Kishorn – Lochcarron – Plockton – Kyle of Lochalsh

Tour length 161 miles

The tour of Wester Ross takes the visitor into the kind of wilderness and remoteness which only mountains can provide. Here, the human element is scaled against these massive ranges and one cannot help the sense of the wonder of Nature which these high peaks engender. Variety is offered by land-locked lochs, whose sparkling waters serve to enhance one's feasting of the eyes. Long arms of the sea stretch far into the land, as though seeking some kind of refuge. Small remote communities, many with less than 100 inhabitants, hint at the special kind of living which is offered in Wester Ross, and which visitors can taste for themselves.

Balmacara

The main road out of Kyle of Lochalsh is the A87 which runs through Balmacara, a quiet settlement where the Balmacara Estate is run by the National Trust for Scotland. Visit the N.T.S. Information Centre and the Lochalsh Woodland Garden for a sight of a wide variety of trees and exotic plants basking in the warmth of the Gulf Stream. Just past Kirkton, the A890 goes northwards. However, a short detour is recommended: keep on the A87 past Dornie and one will see the

Eilean Donan

most photographed castle in Britain: Eilean Donan. The castle is on a site which was occupied by a vitrified fort before the first stronghold was erected in 1230. It was held by the MacRaes as constables to the Earls of Seaforth. It was later garrisoned by Spanish troops who had landed to help the Jacobite cause of the Old Pretender, James, father of Bonnie Prince Charlie. But that affair did not last long and the castle was battered into a ruinous state by an

English warship. It remained like that until 1912 when the plans of the original castle were uncovered and used to effect a complete restoration of the building, which cost a quarter of a million pounds and took twenty years to finish. The result is quite perfect. Bare stone walls show off Chippendale and Sheraton furniture. Timbered roofs support iron chandeliers. The banqueting hall takes one back in time to the days when Highland chiefs were almost omnipotent. Part of the ancient vitrified fort can still be seen.

Return now to the turn-off at Kirkton to join the A890 and on to Stromeferry. This small village once had a small ferry (hence the name) taking passengers across Loch Carron to the Applecross peninsula. Only a few remains can be seen of old Strome Castle, blown up in 1609, the end result of a bitter feud, lasting 100 years, between MacDonnell of Glengarry and the MacKenzies of Kintail. If nothing else, the stones remind one of the turbulent history of the Highlands in times past. The road now skirts the eastern shore of Loch Carron, with the eyes continually raised to the north-west to catch glimpses of the magnificent heights of the Torridon mountains.

The little village of Strathcarron can be passed through save for a backward look down Loch Carron. The road accompanies the railway line northward through moor and woodland to reach Achnasheen, another small Highland community lying under the slopes of Fhionn Bheinn, the White Mountain. It is a favourite centre for hill-climbers. An opportunity should be taken to visit the craft workshop in the village where local gemstones are set in gold and silver. This drive to Achnasheen is a 22-mile run through remote country punctuated only by a few small hamlets, but still accompanied east and west by the high peaks, and crossing the bridges over the many rivers which cut through the moorland like veins.

From Achnasheen the road now goes westward on the A832 into the district known as Torridon, to reach the village of Kinlochewe. Here are some of the oldest rocks in the world. The village lies on the edge of the Beinn Eighe National

Stromeferry

Strathcarron

Achnasheen

Kinlochewe

Nature Reserve, the home of red deer, golden eagle, pine marten and wild cat. Here another decision must be made: take the A896 southward, or continue on the A832 along the shores of Loch Maree to reach Inverewe Gardens. If the latter choice is made it means a 50-mile round trip. But what lies at Inverewe is a literal sight for sore eyes. Despite the grand beauty of this area with mountains and fine, almost unsurpassed coastal scenery, to come upon the extensive gardens at Inverewe is one of the highlights which make any holiday memorable. The gardens were nothing but barren moorland in 1862. But the owner, Osgood MacKenzie, decided that he would create a garden. To do this he had to bring soil in from surrounding areas to provide his trees, plants and shrubs with something to grow in. This soil was carried in nothing more sophisticated than baskets. The idea of creating a garden must have seemed 'daft' to the locals, but MacKenzie persevered, slowly building up a stock of trees to act as wind shelters and then bringing in more varieties of plants and shrubs. The temperate influence of the Gulf Stream played no small part in what is seen today as a most magnificent memorial to a man of vision who was also in love with what Nature can do given a helping hand.

Returning to Kinlochewe, a word might be said about Loch Maree. This piece of water is often claimed to be the loveliest inland loch in Scotland. One can prove this for oneself as one drives along the shore of the loch which is some 15 miles long and dominated by the superb peak of Slioch. Three hundred years ago Isle Maree, one of a small cluster of islands in the loch, was the site of an iron smelting operation. Off the roadside, to the right and at the end of the loch, is the Visitor Centre of the Nature Conservancy which interprets the Beinn Eighe (viewed to the south) area.

Before Kinlochewe, the A896 is taken, to drive into Torridon. Beinn Eighe is now on the right and, farther on, the massif of Liathach, as one drives through Glen Torridon. On the left are the Coulin and Ben Damph forests and a dozen or so red sandstone mountains with white quartzite

Inverewe

Torridon caps. At the foot of the glen is Torridon village where an Information Centre is run by the National Trust for Scotland. The Centre has a display of Highland Wildlife and a Deer Museum. The temptation to stay awhile here should not be resisted if time allows, for this area is unique in Britain, not only for scenery but for beasts and plant life. The village lies at the head of Upper Loch Torridon.

Crossing the River Torridon, the road now runs along the lochside. At Balgy there are Falls where one might be fortunate and see salmon running in season. The coastal scenery makes a welcome change to the mountains. At Shieldaig one finds a peaceful village whose folk combine fishing and crofting activities with catering for a prosperous tourist industry. The road now strikes inland once more. At Kishorn one can see the impact of North Sea Oil development in the form of the oil-platform construction yard, though the small communities of Kishorn and Achintraid seem oblivious of its presence. Lochcarron is strung out along the shore of the loch, with a backcloth of mountains. It was set out in the eighteenth century and was the other terminus of the Strome Ferry. Strathcarron is now reached after which the return drive arrives at Stromeferry. Kyle of Lochalsh can be one's final destination, but if time allows it would be worthwhile to take a short diversion, to include a visit to Plockton. It is the shorter route back to Kyle in any case, even if the road is narrow and one has to use the passing places with care.

Plockton Plockton is a delight. It is yet another settlement laid out in the eighteenth century. It is now a favourite haunt of sailors and is noted for the regatta held each year at the end of July. Nestling in a small bay of Loch Carron, the village has a magnificent view across the bay to wooded crags. Again one comes across semi-tropical trees and shrubs growing as if this were their natural habitat. A short drive now takes us back to Kyle of Lochalsh.

Tour of Isle of Skye

Kyleakin – Broadford – Portree – Dunvegan – Armadale – Kyleakin

Tour length 135 miles

The jumping-off point for the Isle of Skye is Kyle of Lochalsh, and the car ferry crossing takes five minutes. There is always the feeling of expectation when one lands on an island, and Skye offers no exception to this rule. The tour round the island involves just over 100 miles, which is an indication of the extent of Skye, which is some 60 miles long, but has no place on the island more than 5 miles distant from the sea.

The island is deeply cut into a number of peninsulas. For the most part Skye is bare and treeless and almost all of it is devoted to sheep grazing and arable crofting, particularly round the coastal strip. There are some tree plantations, much of it in the form of conifer plantations and run by the Forestry Commission. The district of Sleat, in the south, is perhaps the most pleasant area, with a green and garden-like aspect. The most scenic area is the range of Cuillin mountains, high, bare and majestic peaks which formed the nursery area last century for the sport of hill-climbing which so many follow today. A century ago the Cuillins were in fact more popular with painters than climbers. Turner, MacCulloch, and other eminent British landscape artists found inspiration in these mountains, which suggests they were no mean climbers themselves.

Kyleakin   The stepping-off point on Skye is Kyleakin, a small village with a fishing pier. The ruins of Castle Moil, perched on a hill overlooking the harbour, date from the twelfth century. There is a rather pebbly beach here if one wants to take a stroll along the shore for a few minutes. The road out of Kyleakin runs for some 8 miles to Broadford, passing a number of crofting townships such as Breakish, Waterloo (!) and

Broadford   Harropool. The village of Broadford is surrounded by welcome green fields and is Skye's biggest crofting township. There are good hotels and a good shopping centre here with an excellent view across the water to the Applecross peninsula on the mainland. The road westward

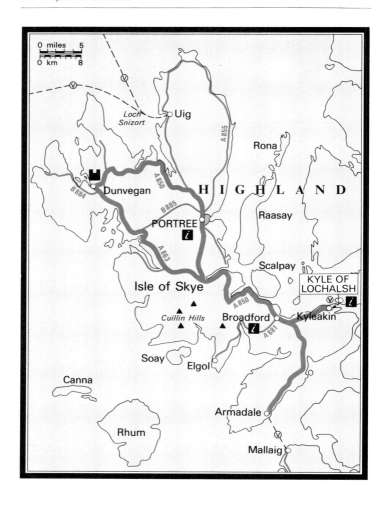

out of Broadford hugs the shore, round Loch Ainort, and then cuts through the area known as Lord MacDonald's Forest. The term forest as used in the Highlands generally means a deer forest, where moorland rather than trees is the dominant feature.

The run beside the shore of Loch Sligachan is impressive for its mountainous backcloth, after which there is a stiff climb (best taken slowly) up into Glen Varragill before the road descends into Portree, the administrative centre for the island. The township was given its name (King's Harbour) because in 1540 King James v landed here to try to end a long-standing bitter feud between the two major clans on Skye, the MacDonalds and the MacLeods. The town also was the scene of the parting between Flora Macdonald and Prince Charlie after she had helped him to escape from South Uist in the Outer Hebrides. The room where they parted is now part of the *Royal Hotel*. The town is a fine, well-developed area with plenty of facilities for relaxation and eating.

Portree

From Portree we take the A850 and continue on this road past Borve to make for Dunvegan, possibly the highlight of any visit to Skye. Dunvegan Castle is reputed to be the oldest inhabited castle in Scotland, the MacLeods having lived here continuously for 700 years. The castle stands on a crag facing the sea, on the site of an old ninth-century Norse fortress. The present structure dates from the fifteenth century, with alterations and additions continued until the middle of the nineteenth century. The castle is open to visitors except on Saturdays and Sundays. There is much of the castle's turbulent past history to see here, including the famous Fairy Flag, the Bratach Sith, which tradition says was given to William, the 4th Chief, by a fairy lover. The flag has been displayed twice to give the MacLeods victory in battle which might have brought disaster to the clan. The third time has yet to come. The woods to the east of the castle were planted in 1780 and make a pleasant change from the barren moors of Skye.

Dunvegan

A tortuous road now goes out of Dunvegan village to make its way along the south coast of this part of Skye to Drynoch where it cuts across to Sligachan to join the road back to Kyleakin. Always the mountain range of the Cuillins dominates the horizon. A couple of miles east of Broadford a right-hand turn takes one to Sleat. The main feature of interest is found at Armadale, where what is left of a once-imposing castle still manages to retain some of its former dignity. Next to the castle is the Clan Donald Centre, devoted to telling the story of the MacDonalds of Sleat. Set in woodlands, this area exudes the atmosphere of former times of comfortable and elegant living. Space has not been available for a fuller picture of Skye to be painted. Suffice it to say that the experience of a visit to the island will be well repaid and make for fond memories, with plenty to tell one's friends.

Armadale

Loch Alsh

Fort William

Tourist Information Centre
Cameron Square, tel 3581

Population 11,079

Cinema
Playhouse, High Street

Places of Interest
West Highland Museum, Cameron Square.

Inverlochy Castle. Just north of the town. The ruins date from the thirteenth century.

Highland Craft Exhibition, High Street. Many items of Highland craft industries are on sale.

Commando Memorial. At Spean Bridge 9 miles north of the town. A memorial to the Commandos of World War Two who trained in the area.

Loch Linnhe. Boating trips on the loch.

Ben Nevis. Easily climbed with suitable clothing and footwear.

As in the American West, the prefix 'fort' indicates a garrison town. Fort William was first established as one of three garrisons to be located in the Highlands (Fort Augustus and Fort George, near Inverness, are the other two) to quell the unruly Highlanders who have always throughout history played games of brinkmanship with successive British governments. The first fortified structure was built as a strong fence and earthworks by General Monk in 1650, acting for Oliver Cromwell. Forty years later the fort was strengthened and named 'Fort William' after the then King William III. The fort received the attention of the Jacobites in 1715 and again in 1745, when 'Bonnie Prince Charlie' tried to regain the British Crown for the Stuarts.

The fort was demolished when the West Highland Railway appeared in 1884, to connect the town to Glasgow. Some five minutes' walk from the Tourist Information Centre, towards the shore of Loch Linnhe, will take the visitor to the remnants of the old fort wall.

The town has a claim to industrial history, for it was here that the first major aluminium reduction plant was built in 1929. The factory's hydro-electric plant is served by water from Loch

Treig some 15 miles distant and carried by pipes which run through the heart of the Ben Nevis range and which can be seen from the main road.

In recent years Fort William has managed to rid itself of its industrial image, to become a major tourist centre, located as it is in the heart of some magnificent scenery and dominated by the bulky mass of Ben Nevis, the highest mountain in Britain.

Much of the historical past of Fort William and the surrounding area, known as Lochaber, can be seen in the West Highland Museum. In particular there are many items of interest relating to the Jacobite Rising of 1745.

As a centre for touring, Fort William is unsurpassed. Not only is it a rail junction with links to Glasgow and Mallaig, but it stands at the southern end of the Caledonian Canal, built in 1822, which makes its way north to Inverness through the three lochs of the Great Glen. It is also the starting point for the 'Road to the Isles' (Rhum, Muck, Eigg and Canna) and the Isle of Skye. Roads link Fort William with the towns of the Spey Valley, north to Inverness, west to the wilderness of Moidart, Ardnumurchan and Morvern, and, of particular interest, the dark and brooding Glen Coe. There are regular bus services to Inverness, Glasgow and Oban. A helicopter service links Fort William with Glasgow (45 minutes) and Oban (15 minutes).

Ben Nevis, despite its forbidding mass, is easily accessible by a well marked path which starts at Achintree Farm in Glen Nevis; an alternative path begins at the Youth Hostel, about 2 miles from the town. The route to the summit is a 4–5 hour trek (3 hours down) and walkers are advised to keep to the standard routes and be well shod and clothed, for Ben Nevis can trap those who are unfamiliar with the mountain. From the summit one can see the Cuillins of Skye and, in exceptionally fine weather, the north-eastern coast of Ireland.

Tour 1

Fort William – Corpach – Glenfinnan – Lochailort – Arisaig – Morar – Mallaig – Roshven – Kinlochmoidart – Acharacle – Salen – Strontian – Inversanda – Corran Ferry – Fort William

Tour length 120 miles

This tour takes the 'Road to the Isles' which runs through some of the most historic and scenic areas of the highlands, comprising mountain and moorland, to the western shores washed by the Sea of the Hebrides. The road is single carriageway which tends to be busy during the summer months. Caution is advised when the road presents 'blind' turns as the route is often used by large lorries carrying fish from Mallaig to markets in the south.

Leave Fort William on the A82 northward and
Banavie   turn left (A830) to Banavie, where the locks join
the southern end of the Caledonian Canal to
Corpach   Loch Linnhe. Corpach is a new sprawling development of housing largely associated with the pulp and paper mill, built in 1966 and since troubled by the industrial recession.

Glenfinnan   Glenfinnan is a major punctuation mark in Scotland's history. The head waters of Loch Shiel look up to the monument erected to commemorate the 'Forty-five' Jacobite Rising. It was at this spot on 19 August 1745 that the standard of Prince Charles Edward was raised to rally the Highland clans in his attempt to reclaim the Crown of Britain for the Stuarts. The monument was erected in 1815. The figure of the Highlander on top of the column is not Prince Charles, as popularly believed. The monument in fact commemorates 'Those who fought and bled in that arduous enterprise' – those Highland clansmen who paid so dearly the price of the Prince's hopes.

The Visitor Centre is run by the National Trust for Scotland and is mainly devoted to telling the

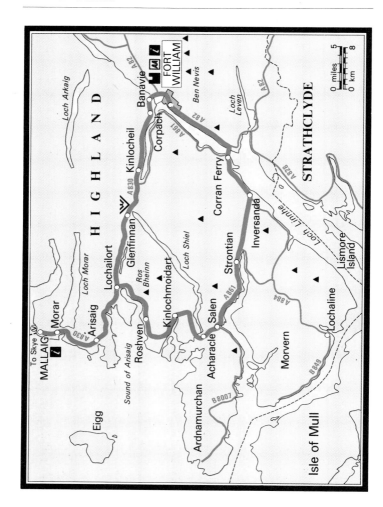

story of the Rising which ended so tragically at the Battle of Culloden in April 1746. Loch Shiel is thought to be among the most beautiful of Scottish lochs. An opportunity to test this is offered by a cruise in a launch which plies the length of the loch in the summer months.

Lochailort   The small village of Lochailort lies at the head of Loch Ailort, one of the fingers of sea which penetrate landwards into this serrated peninsula. The name is derived from the Norse and means 'Deep Fiord'. About six miles on, the road skirts the shores of Loch nan Uamh (Loch of the Caves). A cairn beside the road marks the spot where Prince Charles Edward landed in 1745 and where, a year later, he embarked on the *L'Heureux*, leaving Scotland and his dashed hopes for France and exile.

Arisaig   From Arisaig the road turns north and runs along a shoreline stranded by white sands, the Sands of Morar, derived from white silica. From the road the islands of Muck, Eigg and Rhum can be seen. Past Portnaluchaig there is a nine-hole golf course, offering a welcome, if not unusual, break in the tour.

Morar   Morar Bay is very popular with tourists. The sands here dry out a long way when the tide is on the ebb. Inland, about a quarter of a mile, Loch Morar presents one of Scotland's geological freaks. It reaches 987 feet deep, and though it lies close to shallow seas to the west, there is no other equivalent depth until the Continental Shelf dips into the Antlantic 170 miles north-west between St Kilda and Rockall. Loch Morar is said to be the home of 'Morag', a sister to 'Nessie', the Loch Ness monster. Many sightings of a strange beast have been reported over the years. As with 'Nessie', no conclusive evidence has yet been presented to verify its existence in the deepest inland water in Britain.

Mallaig   Mallaig is one of the major fishing ports on the west coast of Scotland and only came into existence when it was established as the terminus of the West Highland Railway, at the beginning of the century. The piers are crowded with activity when the fishing boats unload catches of herring, mackerel, white fish, prawns and lobsters. It is difficult to imagine that in 1900

Mallaig was a tiny village with fewer than 100 people. In recent years its population of 1,000 people were told that their efforts over the years had made the town one of the foremost ports in Europe for its size. Mallaig is the jump-off port for the Isle of Skye on the car ferry across the Sound of Sleat to Armadale (journey time is 30 minutes). Excursions in small craft are offered during the summer months which take the visitor into some of the nearby sea-lochs. From Mallaig, too, there are ferry services to the islands of Canna, Eigg, Rhum and Muck.

Returning from Mallaig, the southward turning off the road (A861) takes the visitor into Moidart and some of the most sparsely populated areas of Scotland. This road runs through rocky coastal Roshven scenery. Roshven takes its name from the mountain range of Rois-bheinn (red mountain), whose six peaks overlook Loch Ailort. At Millhouse one can see seven beech trees standing by the lochside. These were planted to commemorate the 'Seven Men of Moidart' who accompanied Bonnie Prince Charlie from France in 1745.

Kinlochmoidart Kinlochmoidart House, at the head of Glen Moidart, was once the seat of the MacDonalds of Glenaladale, a family which was second to none in all the Highlands in its support for the Jacobite cause. It was a descendant of this family who erected the monument at Glenfinnan.

Before the road crosses Shiel Bridge, a turn-off to the right takes one to Dorlin with a view of the fourteenth-century Castle Tioram in a reasonable state of preservation despite its age. Acharacle Acharacle (A861) presents a pleasant stop for stretching the legs. The name is derived from the Gaelic (Ath Thorcuil) for Torquil's Ford, where a Norse Viking fell in battle over 1,000 years ago. History lives long in the Highland memory. At Salen Salen the road to the west (B8007) is a minor route into the peninsula of Ardnamurchan (Gaelic: Point of the Great Ocean), at the tip of which is a lighthouse marking the most westerly point on the British mainland. En route can be seen Mingary Castle, another Highland stronghold dating from the thirteenth century and once the venue of a Court of King James IV of Scotland who, in 1495, received the submission of the Lord of the Isles and other island chiefs. The event marked the end of the Lordship of the Isles, a Gaelic-based political unit which was strong enough to make treaties with the English kings.

The road eastward from Salen (A861) skirts Loch Sunart and runs through woods of scrub oak, ash and birch, with new viewpoints at almost every bend in the run. The little crofting

Strontian village of Strontian has a claim to fame in the element strontium, first discovered here in 1764. It is used in the manufacture of fireworks, and burns with a brilliant crimson flame. A nature trail leads to the old lead mines which once provided the metal for the bullets used in the Napoleonic Wars. The mines were worked by French prisoners during that period. Close by Strontian is Ariundle Oakwood Forest Reserve, which contains species of trees that once covered much of Scotland.

In 1843 when a split appeared in the Church of Scotland, known as 'The Disruption', the adherents of the new breakaway Church were refused land on which to build a structure of their own in which to worship. So they asked a Glasgow shipyard to quote for a floating church which was duly delivered and anchored in Loch Sunart. The worshippers were ferried to and from the vessel by small boats. 'The church sank one inch for every 100 people in the congregation', says a description of the times. The vessel was eventually driven ashore in a storm, but was used regularly until permission was given to build a stone church, consecrated in 1873.

Eastward from Strontian the road runs through
Inversanda Glen Tarbert to Inversanda, through open moorland flanked by the mass of Creach Bheinn on the south side. From the shores of Loch Linnhe the Appin hills can be seen as one of the many panoramic views which tend to be commonplace
Corran Ferry in this part of the Highlands. At Corran the ferry takes cars across the $\frac{1}{4}$-mile narrow neck which separates lower and upper Loch Linnhe. Though the crossing takes some five minutes, the passage may be rough at times when the fast tide-race goes through the narrows in high winds. Once across, the road (A82) goes north for 14 miles to Fort William.

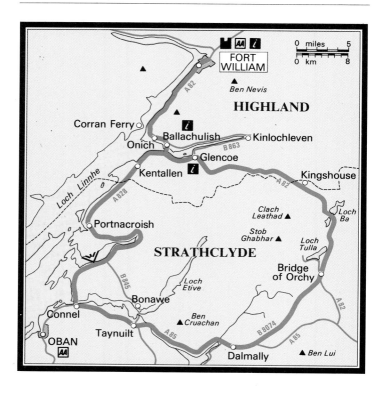

Tour II

Fort William – Onich – Ballachulish – Glencoe – Kingshouse – Bridge of Orchy – Dalmally – Taynuiilt – Bonawe – Connel – Portnacroish – Ballachulish – Fort William

Tour length 120 miles

This route takes the visitor first through some of the magnificent and breath-taking mountains and glens of the southern Grampian Highlands. Some of this route is almost fearsome in its impression of remoteness, particularly if the day is dull. But to compensate for this aspect, there is a feeling of exhilarating freedom: the real world seems to be in another place. The tour can almost be an exercise in opening up the mind and letting the fullness of Nature take over in a most refreshing way. The latter part of this route drives northward along the shores of Loch Linnhe. Mountains, moors and lochs, wooded hillsides and seascapes all combine to fix in the mind one of the attractions of this part of west Scotland: the wilderness which is within comfortable and perhaps reassuring reach of civilisation.

The A82 runs south out of Fort William down the side of the head of Loch Linnhe, along its densely wooded shore. Across the loch are the impressive mountains of Appin and Ardgour. The little village of Onich is a sun-trap with the lowest rainfall anywhere in the Lochaber area. There is here a pleasant clean, if stony, beach. At Ballachulish there is one of the recent blessings bestowed on the Highlands: the bridge across the narrows of Loch Leven, which now saves a 16-mile journey round by Kinlochleven, an industrial village badly planned by being forever out of the sun and overshadowed by the surrounding mountains. On the little island in Loch Leven is the burial place of some of the Macdonalds of

Glencoe, victims of the infamous massacre of 1692, of which more later.

Glencoe   The A82 runs left into Glencoe. To the left one's eyes are literally raised to the mountains of Glencoe. Although the main road bypasses Glencoe village, the visitor is advised to spend a little time in this community dwarfed by its mountain backcloth. Just off the main road at the west end of Glencoe is the Information Centre run by the National Trust for Scotland. Here one is skilfully and sympathetically introduced to the geology, wildlife and history of this part of the Highlands. Glencoe has earned an unenviable place in Scottish history for the murders which were committed in February 1692 when, on the orders of the British Government, soldiers, who had for a few days enjoyed the hospitality of the Macdonalds of Glencoe, attacked their hosts and killed 40 members of the MacIan clan. MacIan had failed to register in time his oath of allegience to King William III. Those in the government decided that an example should be made of clans who were inclined to rebel against the reigning king and who had previously supported the Stewart kings. Through no fault of his own, MacIan was delayed in getting to Inveraray where his declaration was accepted and sent to Edinburgh, only to be rejected as being six days late. One day later orders were given for the whole of the MacIan clan to be destroyed, root and branch. MacIan and his wife died in the massacre and even babes in arms and old men over eighty years of age were not spared. The massacre remains a blot of sombre hue in the history of Scotland and the Highlands.

On from Glencoe the road runs through country which is wild but has a rugged grandeur. At Altnafeadh one looks to the right to the masses of the Big Herdsmen, Buachaille Etive Mor and Beag, guarding the clefted glen which runs to Dalness for 4 miles. Possibly the best view is **Kingshouse** farther along the road at *Kingshouse Hotel*, which is Scotland's oldest inn, situated on the River Etive a short way off the main road. A turn-off to the right leads to the ski lift and ski run. Even if one is not interested in skiing, the lift makes a worthwhile trip to the plateau where one can enjoy the thrill of the high hills. The A82 now runs through Glen Etive, which is 10 miles long.

It is now a straight drive past the dark waters of Loch Ba to the left, on the edge of the desolate Moor of Rannoch, one of the most remote areas of country in the British Isles, crossed only by the Glasgow–Fort William railway. The railway line was built on large bundles of tree trunks to allow it to 'float' on the boggy ground.

Bridge of Orchy   The little community of Bridge of Orchy is a centre for fishing, stalking, mountaineering and skiing. Just south of the village the B8074 runs through the 12 miles of Glen Orchy, following the course of the River Orchy, and joins the A85 into

Dalmally   Dalmally. The village is set a mile or so back from Loch Awe. Near the north side of the *Dalmally Hotel*, on an island in the River Orchy, is a small church. Set among trees, it is an excellent example of an eighteenth-century round church, though in fact it is octagonal with a square tower and spirelets.

Standing on a spit of land at the head of Loch Awe is Kilchurn Castle, which was built in 1440. From whatever angle the structure is viewed it makes an impressive sight. Standing as it does at the foot of magnificent glens and mountains, it was a favourite scene for landscape artists. The Lakeland poet Wordsworth found the scene sufficiently inspiring to write a poem on Kilchurn:

Child of loud-throated war! the mountain stream
Roars in thy hearing; but thy hour of rest
Is come and thou art silent in thy age,
Save when the winds sweep by ...

The road runs along the River Awe into Taynuilt through the Pass of Brander. To the right is the mass of Ben Cruachan on which there is a hydro-electric reservoir and power station built in the heart of the mountain. A visitor centre beside the road displays information about the scheme. One can join tours in a minibus to take one into the power station, which resembles a cathedral.

Taynuilt   The pleasant village of Taynuilt was an

eighteenth-century centre for iron-smelting, using charcoal derived from the extensive oak and beech woods which then covered the district. There is here a monument unique in the Highlands: a memorial to Lord Nelson. The reason for its presence here is the large numbers of Englishmen who were imported for employment at the iron furnaces. When news of Nelson's victory and death at Trafalgar in 1805 reached Taynuilt, the men erected a large standing stone to commemorate the event. It predates the monument in London's Trafalgar Square by 37 years.

Bonawe   The village of Bonawe, Taynuilt's neighbour, was also a centre of the iron-smelting industry, which is said to have been so productive that it supplied all the cannon balls used by the British fleet at Trafalgar. The old furnace has been restored and is worth a visit.

Connel   The A85 now runs for 7 miles to Connel, where the small church is a miniature version of Iona Cathedral. The waters of Loch Etive here tumble over each other as they flow across a ledge of rock at ebb-tide. Though they are called the Falls of Lora, they are in fact simply rapids. The narrows here, just 1 mile from the sea, are spanned by a cantilever bridge which carried the railway line to Ballachulish until it was closed in 1966. It is now used for traffic. We cross it to take the A828 northward past the little villages of Ledaig, New Selma and Barcaldine, where a factory turns dried seaweed (gathered on the shores of the islands of the Hebrides and Orkney) into a bewildering range of products used in such items as ice-cream and cosmetics. About 4 miles on, the road turns round the head of Loch Ceran and one is afforded a view of Castle Stalker, the Castle of the Hunter. It was built in the thirteenth century as the ancient home of the Stewarts of Appin, and has seen much bloody history both inside its walls and in its environs. The castle is now being restored. The neighbour-

Portnacroish   ing village of Portnacroish is a pleasant spot. The island seen to the south is Lismore (Gaelic: Great Garden) which has long been reputed for its fertility, which was probably the reason for its popularity in older times, for it had three castles.

The road now runs through the wooded coast, passing Duror and Kentallen and skirting the foot of Ben Bheithir, which has two shapely tops. This area of Appin featured in the novel *Kidnapped* by Robert Louis Stevenson. This was the scene, too, of the Appin Murder, in which Colin Campbell, known as the 'Red Fox', was shot by unknown hands. Suspicion fell on a man called James Stewart, James of the Glens, who was arrested with no evidence. He was tried before a packed jury of Campbells, who were only too glad to score against a Stewart, a member of a clan which had openly supported the Jacobite cause. The verdict of death was passed and James of the Glens was hanged at Ballachulish. A large stone to his memory is to be seen beside the old ferry slip at Ballachulish, which has an inscription: 'In memory of James Stewart of Acharn, who was executed on this spot on 8th November 1752 for a crime of which he was not guilty'.

From Ballachulish, the A82 runs along the wooded shores of Loch Linnhe back into Fort William.

Oban

Tourist Information Centre
Argyll Square, tel 3122, 3551

Population 8,134

Theatres
Corran Halls, Corran Esplanade
Dunollie Halls, Breadlane Street

Cinema
Phoenix, Albany Terrace

Places of Interest
Dunollie Castle. Thirteenth-century stronghold of the MacDougalls; now in fragments.

McCaig's Folly. A large uncompleted circular structure set on a hill above the town.

The Pier. A busy place with fishing boats and ferries.

Kerrera Island. Set in Oban Bay (5-minute crossing), it has many Norse and Viking associations. Gylen Castle, destroyed by Cromwell's troops in 1645, is in ruins.

The Dog Stone. Beside the War Memorial. By tradition this is the stone to which the Celtic mythological hero Fingal used to tether his hunting dog Bran.

St Columba's Cathedral. An impressive building designed by Sir Giles Scott, on the western side of the town.

As a holiday centre, the west Highland town of Oban seems to offer everything, which is as it should be, simply because much effort has gone into developing Oban and its environs into a base for visitors which they might well feel reluctant to leave. Travel services include road, rail, sea and air facilities, the latter being for small aircraft which land at Connel, some 5 miles north of the town. The railway links Oban with Glasgow. Sea links include both passenger and car ferries to the Inner and Outer Hebrides. There are also local sea services offering trips which make a pleasant change from land-based visits to places of scenic beauty and historical interest. Bus services are comprehensive and extend not only locally but to both Glasgow and Edinburgh.

Entertainment facilities include a cinema, theatre shows, and hotel entertainment which usually takes the form of 'ceilidhs' where the emphasis is on Scottish singing and dancing.

Oban came into its own as a holiday resort when the railway line from Glasgow was completed last century. Today, though tourism is the town's main economic base, local industry also has a place in the form of fishing, a tweed mill and a whisky distillery. The town is built on a site which has had a long association with human habitation. The main street, George Street, runs now where some caves were discovered a century ago containing the remains of Azilian Man (6000 BC). These Middle Stone Age people are thought to have migrated from Europe after Britain became an island.

Among the town's features of interest is McCaig's Folly. This uncompleted structure is a miniature of the Colosseum in Rome, and was an idea of a local banker last century to alleviate the unemployment in the town. It stands on a wooded hill and can be reached from George Street, by way of Craigard Road. The view from here, across to the Island of Mull, is quite something. Another viewpoint is Pulpit Hill, above the south harbour. St Columba's cathedral is one of the few such buildings in the world built entirely of pink granite. For something unusual to see, visit the factory of Oban Glass, where one can see the creation of beautiful objects from such a simple basic material as glass.

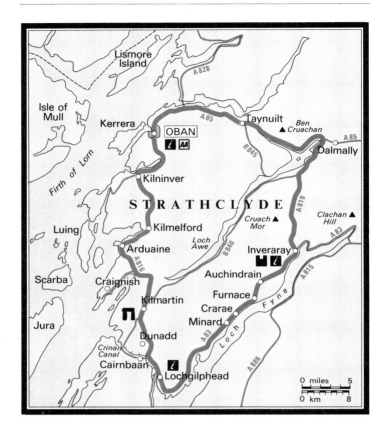

Tour of Southern Argyll

Oban – Kilninver – Kilmelford – Arduaine – Craignish – Kilmartin – Dunadd – Lochgilphead – Minard – Crarae – Furnace – Auchindrain – Inveraray – Oban

Tour length 100 miles

This route takes in some of the magnificent, and accessible, coastal scenery of southern Argyll. Vistas, looking out to sea, offer tantalising glimpses of some of the islands of the Inner Hebrides, including Jura (the Island of Deer), Colonsay and Tiree, though the latter is so flat that only good clear weather will make it visible as a thickening of the horizon. Some of the area of South Lorn is deeply indented by long arms of the sea. The route cuts across the twinned peninsulas of Knapdale and the Mull of Kintyre to the shores of Loch Fyne, still famed for the excellence of its herring. The route passes through the cradle of the distant origins of Scotland before she became a nation of united races. More recent history can be seen in Inveraray Castle, possibly the highlight of the tour, and the present seat of the Dukes of Argyll. Following a disastrous fire some years ago, the damage has now been repaired and the castle basks in the glory it justly deserves.

Kilninver The road south out of Oban is the A816. About a mile before the village of Kilninver on the near shore of Loch Feochan is a natural rock pier known as Creag na Marbh (Gaelic: Rock of the Dead). At this rock galleys used to wait to carry the dead kings of Scotland over to Iona for burial in St Oran's graveyard. If one takes the minor road B844, a 4-mile run reaches the quaint hump-backed Clachan Bridge, which spans the Atlantic over to the island of Seil. It was built in 1792 by Thomas Telford, many of whose civil engineering works the visitor meets in any tour of Scotland. The single stone arch rises some 40 feet above the waters of Seil Sound to allow ships to pass under it. Seil island was once the scene of a busy slate industry which gave prosperity to the local community for two centuries until it collapsed when the sea flooded into the mines.

Back on the A816 once more, the road now goes through Glen Gallain. If a delightful scent reaches one's nostrils it is more than likely from the wild thyme which grows along the roadside in abundance. To the left rises Carn Dearg, Red Hill. Once through the deep ravine of the Pass of Melfort the road runs into Kilmelford village. This area has many delightful scenic features, including rivers and lochs which make it a fisherman's paradise. In former days salmon were so plentiful that they were caught as they ran up rivers. Every household in the district was able to lay in a barrel of salted salmon for use during the hungry winter months. Nearby sea-loch Melfort has no sandy bays but offers a pleasant walk along its north shore through scrub birch and ash. At the southern tip of Loch Melfort is Arduaine, situated on a promontory. Arduaine House was for many years the seat of the Campbells of Arduaine. The plants and trees in the delightful gardens benefit from the warmth of the Gulf Stream.

At the head of Loch Craignish, a minor road (B8002) runs to Craignish Castle, originally a stronghold of the Clan MacDougall, then occupied by the Clan Campbell. Again one meets the wonder of west-coast gardens. Here a rhododendron garden, a shrub native to the Himalayas, flourishes. Looking directly out to sea from the castle is the Gulf of Corrievreckan, where two tidal races meet to create whirlpools which have claimed many small boats.

Continuing on the A816, the road goes through the pass of Bealach Mor, the Great Pass. From here, at a suitable vantage point, the view west is of Loch Craignish with all its wooded islets and rocks seeming to choke back any progress of the sea. The road now goes inland for a few miles to reach the village of Kilmartin. Before it is reached, at the junction with the B840, is Carnasserie Castle. Sitting on top of a grassy hill, it is an example of a sixteenth-century fortified house, once the home of Bishop Carswell, who printed the first book in the Gaelic language in 1567. Still in a very fair state of preservation, there is much to see of interest. The

Kilmelford

Arduaine

Craignish

Kilmartin

open fireplace in the kitchen is big enough for the roasting of a whole ox. This whole area is full of historic and prehistoric remains. If what is left of Kilmartin Castle does not excite interest, then attention turned to Kilmartin churchyard will definitely reward. The church itself is perched on the breast of a hill. Here are two rare carved stone crosses, the earlier (with the Celtic patterns) dating from the twelfth century. Many of the ancient sculptured gravestones are protected from the weather by a glass-roofed building. Here also are the Poltalloch stones, gravestones of the Malcolm chiefs. Close by, on the banks of the River Add, are Bronze Age chambered cairns.

Dunadd About 3 miles south of Kilmartin, on the western side of the A816, lies Dunadd, a shallow valley which is one of the richest repositories in Scotland of prehistoric structures, burial cairns and standing stones, all bearing witness to thousands of years of continuous occupation. Dunadd was once the capital of Dalriada, one of the early kingdoms in Scotland (c. 850–500 BC). Here kings held court and were crowned. Tradition has it that one king, Fergus, brought with him from Ireland the stone used by Jacob the Israelite as a pillow. This stone had previously been held in Cashel Cathedral in Ireland and was used at the coronation of Irish kings, where it was known as the Lia Fail (Stone of Destiny). After Fergus took it to Dunadd, it was given a similar role, until it was removed to the town of Scone, where Edward I of England, in 1296, captured it and carried it off to Westminster Abbey, where it now lies under the Coronation Chair.

The fort of Dunadd is built on a natural hill, which, with its surrounding rocks, shows signs of intensive occupation. Here one can see, carved on stone slabs, a wild boar, along with the imprint of a human foot and a cup-like impression, which might have served as an anointing basin. Tradition says the footprint is that of King Fergus. It was part of the Celtic coronation ceremony that the newly crowned king had to place his foot in the hollow, symbolising an obligation to walk in the steps of his forefathers. This whole area is chock-full of standing stones, cairns, carved stones, vitrified forts, stone circles, old churches and castles. Little wonder it is known as the Cradle of Scotland. All approaches to Dunadd are guarded by no fewer than 70 forts within a 10-mile radius.

Cairnbaan   South of Dunadd is Cairnbaan, close by the Crinan Canal which joins the waters of Loch Gilb (top of Loch Fyne) with those of the Sound of Jura. The canal is crossed by a bridge. Work on the Crinan Canal was started in 1794, but it ran into many problems, both financial and engineering, which were not solved until 1812, when engineer Thomas Telford was called in to complete the work. It is now used mainly for small craft and pleasure boats. There are 15 locks along its 9-mile length.

Lochgilphead   A short run takes us into Lochgilphead. This is a popular holiday centre which is set at the head of Loch Gilp, around which its stone-built houses cluster, all looking south to the distant hills on the Isle of Arran. Lochgilphead is the market town and the administrative centre for mid-Argyll. It offers a chance to stretch one's legs. Loch Gilp is a 3-mile inlet of Loch Fyne and has sandy flats which dry out for quite some distance when the tide is on the ebb.

The A83 runs out eastward from Lochgilphead to follow the shoreline of the upper reaches of Loch Fyne, still famed for its excellent herring, though the days of huge catches are well and truly over, the result of indiscriminate over-fishing of the herring stock. The road runs through a number of small communities to reach

Minard   Minard. This was once a prosperous community with its economy based on quarrying and fishing. Minard Castle, built in the Scots Baronial style,

Crarae   is now a hotel. A little farther on is Crarae where one meets yet another of the excellent west-coast gardens, planned with love and care by Sir George Campbell. Some 33 acres of Glen Crarae have been planted with conifers, rhododendrons, azaleas and many rare shrubs and plants. The gardens are open all year round and are so extensive that one could quite easily spend a whole day just absorbing the pleasure of these excellent surroundings.

Furnace   North of Crarae is the village of Furnace, so

called because it was an important iron-smelting centre in the eighteenth century. Much of the wood required for charcoal was taken from the extensive forests in the area, which still shows the scars of denuded hillsides. When the smelting industry declined, the mills were used to make gunpowder, which industry continued until 1883 when a great explosion destroyed the factory, the remains of which can still be seen.

Auchindrain   At Auchindrain is the museum of country life known as the Auchindrain Farming Township. Much effort has gone into creating the conditions of farming life in the late eighteenth century in the Highlands. A Visitor Centre interprets that life in a number of displays. The croft houses mostly date from about 1770.

Inveraray   The town of Inveraray is an example of eighteenth-century planning, though it has a history which is older than that, being closely tied up with the fortunes of the Clan Campbell and Inveraray Castle. The present castle replaced the fifteenth-century building, some of which can still be seen. It was started in 1746 and completed about fifty years later. Since then various alterations have taken place. The castle has been described as 'an entirety designed to delight the eye from every angle of approach, both by land and by water'. Inside, the castle is no less impressive, being richly decorated, with paintings, furniture, and an armoury hall displaying weapons dating from the fifteenth to the eighteenth century. Part of the castle, not open to the public, is used by the Duke of Argyll, the head of Clan Campbell. Many of the houses in the town have been restored to make the general appearance of Inveraray a delight to the eye. There is, particularly, a very relaxing atmosphere in the town, set against the sweep of the opposite shore of Loch Fyne.

The A819 now runs northward through the wooded Glen Aray to Cladich, where magnificent views of the circle of mountains at this end of Loch Awe can be seen in all their impressive majesty, with Ben Cruachan to the north-west the highest of all. Our tour effectively ends at the Dalmally junction, whence it is a run back through the gloomy Pass of Brander to Oban.

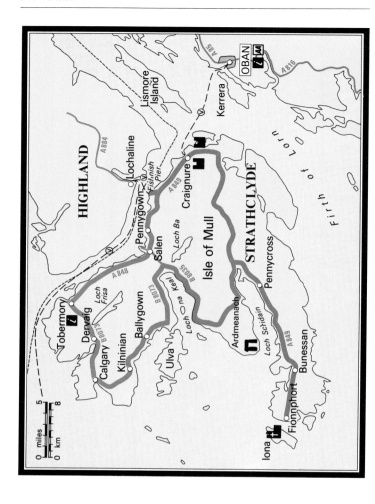

Tour of Isle of Mull and Iona

Craignure – Pennygown – Salen – Tobermory – Dervaig – Calgary – Ballygown – Ardmeanach – Pennycross – Fhionnfhort – Iona – Craignure

Tour length 99 miles

Car ferries operate from Oban each weekday at regular intervals to Craignure (45 minutes) and Tobermory (2 hours). Catamaran passenger services also operate from Oban to these two points. There are internal bus services on the Isle of Mull, again operating on weekdays, which connect with the ferry sailings. There are restricted bus services on Sundays.

The island of Mull is deeply indented by sea lochs, so much so that its coastline is over 300 miles in length. As the road system largely skirts the island, many opportunities are offered to soak in some of the excellent sea vistas and the magnificent scenery of rugged cliffs. Mull boasts one respectable mountain, Ben Mor, but there are a number of companions whose heights rising above the rolling moorland and hilly areas add that extra dimension of interest to the tour.

Craignure From Craignure, the ferry terminal, the road west is the A849, skirting the southern shore of the Sound of Mull. Across the Sound can be seen the ruggedness of the Morvern peninsula. The Fishnish turn-off at Fishnish leads to the pier where a car ferry crosses (in about 5 minutes depending on the weather) to Lochaline in Morvern. At Pennygown Pennygown, by the roadside and ½ mile east of the Forsa River, is a ruined chapel, where one of the early MacLeans of Duart and his wife practised black magic by roasting cats to summon the devil. The ancient graveyard has many fallen memorials to the long dead. Within the chapel is the broken shaft of an early Celtic cross with excellent carvings of singular beauty. Salen Salen village is by tradition the place where St Columba set foot on Mull on his way to Iona to found the monastery there. On the northern side of Salen Bay is the ruin of Aros Castle, built in the thirteenth century as one of a string of fortifications in the area. It was last used in 1608 when a great banquet was arranged to which all the major Hebridean chiefs were invited. But no sooner had they set foot in the castle than they were arrested and taken to Edinburgh to swear to King James VI to change their unruly and piratical habits. Salen was founded by the 'father of Australia', Lachlan MacQuarrie, when he retired as Governor of New South Wales. He died at his House of Grulin, above the shore of Loch na Keal, where his mausoleum draws many Australian visitors.

The road north from Salen, past Aros Castle, offers an excellent taste of the eastern part of Mull, particularly from the high ground above Tobermory Bay. In sympathetic weather one can see the mass of Ben Cruachan, only one feature of the spectacular horizon to the north, on Morvern, and east to the mainland. A pair of binoculars is essential to appreciate fully the panoramic views one gets in any part of the Highlands.

Tobermory   The 'capital' of Mull is Tobermory (Gaelic: Well of St Mary). It clusters, as if at the behest of a photographer, round the bay, sheltered by Calve Island. Screened from wind as it is by the Morvern peninsula, it is one of the safest anchorages on the west coast of Scotland. Little wonder it is a mecca for yachtsmen, who hold an annual regatta each August. It was founded in 1788 as a fishing port, but that activity has long been overtaken by tourism as its main economic base.

Out in the bay is the wreck of a Spanish galleon, one of the ill-fated ships from the Armada invasion of England in 1588. The ship is the *Florida*, which made for the bay to seek shelter. The Spaniards were well received by the local folk, who supplied the ship with fresh stores. But when it seemed that payment was not forthcoming, so local tradition has it, a Donald MacLean was sent aboard, who managed to set a fuse in the ship's armoury and escaped before it blew up. Another story suggests that there was a

rumour that the ship had treasure amounting to
£30,000 in gold coin and this attracted the
ambitions of some people. The *Florida* is now
under about 60 feet of water and is covered with
clay. Many attempts have been made to recover
the ship's fittings and treasure, but so far only a
few coins, silver goblets and brass cannon have
been found.

Tobermory is a pleasant place to relax in. The
eighteenth-century houses are a visual attraction, with their pointed attics and walls painted
cream, white and pink. There is a sense of civic
pride and well-being here which is quite con-
tagious. The Mull and Iona Folk Museum has
displays relating to local history. From
Tobermory a steamer can take one to the islands
of the Inner Hebrides, three times weekly, to
Coll, Tiree, and out to Barra and South Uist in
the Western Isles.

Dervaig
From Tobermory the road (B8073) goes southward a distance of 6 miles to Dervaig, a small
settlement which has a modern round tower and
a group of standing stones. It was to Dervaig, in
the old days, that cattle from the Western Isles
were taken, to be driven across Mull to
Grasspoint, before being shipped to Oban, to
begin a long trek to the cattle markets at Falkirk
and Crieff. The Old Byre Museum, 1 mile south of
Dervaig, is devoted to the theme of crofting life
on Mull. At Dervaig is possibly Britain's smallest
theatre, run by Barrie and Marianne Hesketh,
who have converted a barn to seat 45 people.
Productions are quite spectacular, with both
actors capable of displaying an astonishing
range of theatrical gifts. For those interested in
the theatre, the Heskeths' performances are a
'must'. Phone Dervaig 267 to book a seat.

Calgary
Five miles on from Dervaig is Calgary. It was
emigrants from Calgary, Mull, who settled in
Canada in 1883 and gave their settlement the
same name. Such is Highland nostalgia. Here is
the only shell-sand beach in west Mull, and it
stretches in generous quantity with most of the
desirable trimmings: a sweep of green machair,
wooded hill-slopes and bold outer cliffs. The road
now turns round from Treshnish Point past Burg,
where there can be seen traces of an Iron Age

fort (on the seaward side of the road), and on to Kilninian. An old burial ground here displays a fine carved medieval slab. At Ballygown the remains of an Iron Age tower or broch can be seen. The islands facing this side of Mull are Gometra and Ulva. Ulva island was the birthplace of the grandfather of David Livingstone, the Scottish explorer and missionary. He was one of the party who secretly removed the body of James of the Glens (see p. 131) from the gibbet to give it a decent burial in Old Duror Church. General Lachlan MacQuarrie was also born on Ulva. As mentioned earlier, the general's mausoleum can be seen at Grulin, at the head of Loch na Keal.

The road now heads south to cross the Ardmeanach peninsula. The headland of this area is called 'The Wilderness'. The southern half is in the care of the National Trust for Scotland. Here there is a geological wonder: implanted on the cliff-face is a high fossil tree, engulfed by lava flow some 50 million years ago. Visitors are warned that to reach this curio entails a hard, long and rough walk over mud, rock and bog.

The end of the B8035 joins the better road of the A849 for a trip to Iona, along the shore of Loch Scridain. At Pennycross (sometimes called Pennyghael) there is a good restaurant and bar for welcome refreshment. A memorial cross can be seen here, erected in memory of the family of Beatons who, for 300 years, were physicians to the MacLeans of Duart. Bunessan was a naval base during the last World War. The last leg of this road ends at Fhionnphort (pronounced Finnafort). Here one must leave the car to take passenger ferry across to Iona.

All the main sites on the island are within walking distance. Iona was the cradle of Christianity in the West Highlands. Here it was that St Columba founded his monastery, now developed over the centuries into a magnificent cathedral, surrounded by reminders of the ancient past, in particular St Oran's cemetery, where are buried 48 Scottish, 8 Norwegian, 4 Irish and 2 French kings. It is reputed to be the oldest Christian burial place in Scotland.

Marginal notes: Kilninian, Ballygown, Ardmeanach, Pennycross, Bunessan, Fhionnphort, Iona

Much of Iona Cathedral has been restored in recent decades and it now exudes, despite the presence of numerous visitors, the atmosphere of a holy place which it once had. There is so much to see on Iona that the best suggestion may be to obtain some literature and choose places to visit according to one's interests.

The road back to Craignure passes Torosay and Duart castles. The former is a nineteenth-century building, with an excellent collection of pictures. Duart Castle dates from the thirteenth century and now, restored by Sir Fitzroy MacLean, houses many historic relics of the Clan MacLean. For those interested in Scouting, there is a comprehensive exhibition of the movement.

A mile or so past Torosay is Craignure, reached in time for the ferry back to Oban.

Dunoon

Tourist Information Centre
Pier Esplanade, tel 3785

Population 9,372

Theatre
Queen's Hall, Main Street

Cinema
Studio A, John Street

Places of Interest
Castle Gardens. Contain ruins of a thirteenth-century castle.

Highland Mary Statue. On Castle Hill.

Morag's Fairy Glen. At the end of the West Bay.

Younger Botanic Gardens. Seven miles north-west of Dunoon.

Castle House. Houses the Tulloch Library (1822).

Moot Hill. West of Castle Hill. It was once the place of arbitrary justice administered to wrong-doers.

Dunoon is the main town in that part of southern Argyll called Cowal, which is one of the most interesting of the many peninsulas in the area, for it offers such a variety of scenery that one could call it 'Scotland in miniature'. There are vast forests, moorland, wooded lochs, mountains of respectable heights and, as if this were not enough for one area, there is the sea, which drives its lochs deep into the land. Cowal has been developed over the years to cater for tourists, yet it is not so fully exploited that the visitor cannot enjoy plenty of peace and quiet to relax the mind in the solitude which many wilderness places offer.

Dunoon began its role as a holiday resort for Glasgow folk in 1779, the year in which a Glasgow family made the safari (for such were the conditions in those days for travelling) to the town. From then the word got round that Dunoon was a place not to be missed and since then it has earned its reputation for making tourists welcome. Just up from the pier (where there are car-ferry connections to Gourock – 20 minutes) there are the Castle Gardens, which are flood-lit at night and present a fairyland scene. On Castle Hill is the statue of Mary Campbell, the 'Highland Mary' lover of Robert Burns. The statue looks towards Ayrshire, the county in which Burns lived and worked to become Scotland's national poet. Within the Gardens is the

Queen's Hall, one of the finest theatres on the Clyde coast, offering light entertainment during the summer months. It is only when one begins to walk Dunoon's sea front that one becomes aware of how long this sea-girt promenade is: 4 miles! But it is a worthwhile walk. Just north of Dunoon and linked with it by the promenade is Kirn, which is a popular harbour with yachtsmen. In August of each year Dunoon is the venue of the Cowal Highland Gathering at which hundreds of Highland dancers, pipers and pipe bands compete. It is an event once experienced, never forgotten.

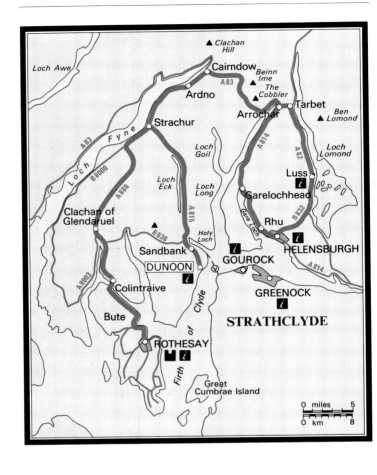

Dunoon – Sandbank – Strachur – Ardno – Cairndow – Arrochar – Tarbet – Luss – Helensburgh – Rhu – Garelochead – Strachur – Colintraive – Rothesay (Isle of Bute) – Dunoon

Tour length 124 miles; with Rothesay 148 miles

This is mainly a scenic route, but one with such variety that one will be tempted often to 'stop and stare', and simply soak in mountain peaks, woods, tree-lined lochs, seascapes, glens and the dappled waters of the many small lochs which ripple with rising trout. The route includes the western shore of Loch Lomond, a household name for beauty. A visit to the Isle of Bute and Rothesay can be taken in to sample what this area can offer. The historic past of Cowal shows its many faces, from Viking times. There are long stretches of easy and comfortable driving on good roads, which adds to the pleasure of the route.

Take the road north out of Dunoon round by Kirn, Hunter's Quay and the southern shore of the Holy Loch, the latter so called because a ship was wrecked in the loch with a cargo of earth from the Holy Land, destined for the foundations of Glasgow Cathedral. The loch is now an American naval base. The road joins the A885 Sandbank at Sandbank, where many fine yachts are built, including the Americas Cup challengers *Sovereign* and *Sceptre*. From Sandbank the road Loch Eck continues (A815) along the eastern shore of Loch Eck. This water is a deep trough some 6 miles long, hedged in by heavily wooded hills which lend a rather sombre atmosphere to the scene. However, if the sun is shining, the loch assumes a quite different character. Some delightful picnic spots offer the temptation to stop and sit awhile. Across the loch the clean-cut craggy heights of Beinn Mhor make an impressive sight.

At the northern end of Loch Eck is Glenbranter Forest, once the home of the famous Scots comedian Sir Harry Lauder, at whose door the exaggerated caricature of the Scot (kilt and twisted walking stick) has been laid. He was, however, something of an ambassador for Scotland during his lifetime. On a low hill on the right of the road is a memorial obelisk erected by Sir Harry to his son who was killed in the First World War. He received the news when on stage in London and sang to the audience, unaware of his son's death, the popular song of the time: *Keep right on to the end of the Road*. The church at Strachur is of interest. Erected in 1787, it has old sculptured stones built into its walls.

Strachur

Proceeding north on the A815 the road skirts the eastern side of Loch Fyne, across which one can catch a sight of Inveraray. At Ardno there is a Stone Age relic known as the Ardno Cairn. The road leading off to the east above Ardno goes through Hell's Glen, and passes the head of Loch Goil and, eventually, the stately ruin of Carrick Castle, dating from the fifteenth century. The end of the A815 joins the A83 at Cairndow. Close by are the Strone Gardens where the tallest tree in Scotland is said to grow. At Cairndow is the inn where the poet Keats ended up after a long and exhausting walk across the Rest and Be Thankful. He scratched his name on a window pane in his bedroom. Cairndow is a pleasant village on the shore of Loch Fyne. An attractive feature is the uniquely shaped white church built in 1815, a target for any camera. To the south-west of the village is Ardkinglas House and its marvellous gardens.

Ardno

Cairndow

The A83 is now taken through Glen Kinglas. This glen, with Glen Croe, links the long sea lochs of Fyne and Long. The road winds its way to the bare and rather windy Pass of Rest and Be Thankful, so called because the army of the eighteenth century were more than pleased to have finished the long and hard job of repairing the road. One can also appreciate why Keats was so glad to reach the hospitality of the inn at Cairndow. To the left is Ben Arthur or 'The Cobbler'. Again there is the overwhelming evidence of the presence of the Forestry Commission which has clothed the lower slopes with Sitka and Norway spruce. In winter this pass funnels winds to blasts of enormous velocity, which have often overturned large lorries and forced buses off the road.

Arrochar   Arrochar lies at the northern tip of Loch Long. It is a busy road junction and is a popular jumping-off point for those interested in hill-walking and climbing. Some 2 miles farther on is Tarbet village. In the year 1263, King Hakon of Norway, in his last attempt to hold on to his lands on the west coast of Scotland, ordered his men to drag galleys across the land from the shore of Loch Long into Loch Lomond to lay waste the communities inaccessible by sea. At Tarbet one can get the best view of Ben Lomond.

Loch Lomond   Loch Lomond is probably the best-known piece of water in the world and is the largest piece of fresh water in Britain. The visitor, however, may well be a bit disappointed because the hills run down to the loch waters rather too closely for any real panoramic views to be had. Even so, the run down the western shore (A82) offers some tantalising glimpses. The road tends to twist and turn as far as Inverbeg and care is needed to keep watch for oncoming traffic. Opposite Luss can be seen the many islands in the loch. Luss itself is a pretty village with the mellow stone of the cottages covered with roses. In the local church there is an effigy (fifteenth century) of St Kessog, who brought Christianity to the area in the sixth century.

South of Luss we take the right-hand turn (B832) which leads into Helensburgh. This is a holiday resort and is the birthplace of John Logie Baird, pioneer of television. Henry Bell is also commemorated at Rhu, adjoining the northern side of Helensburgh. Bell launched *The Comet* in 1812, the first practical passenger steamer in Europe. He is buried near Hill House, Rhu, which was designed by the Glasgow architect Charles Rennie Mackintosh, and contains many examples of his furniture. At Rhu the Glenard Gardens are worth a visit to see the woodlands and flowering shrubs.

The road (A814) runs north along the shore of Gare Loch. All these waters are crammed with Navy ships and the whole area is littered with military installations of one kind or another. The loch was a Combined Operations base during World War Two. The village of Garelochhead lies at the northern tip of the loch. The road now goes northwards to Arrochar, along the eastern shore of Loch Long. Thereafter it is a drive back to Strachur, and Dunoon if one wishes.

A short visit to the Isle of Bute is, however, recommended. Take the A886 south of Strachur and enjoy the long but pleasant drive through Glendaruel. The glen begins at Strathlachlan with views of brown moorland which give way to woodlands, after which the glen opens out to a strath. The old bridge across the River Ruel was the scene in AD 1110 of a battle between the Scots and Norwegians commanded by the son of King Magnus Barefoot. The Scots won the day and celebrated by throwing the bodies of the Vikings into the river, whence came its name, Red Water.

The road ends at Colintraive. Here one takes the car ferry across the Kyles of Bute to the Isle of Bute. The name Colintraive is derived from 'The Strait of Swimming', from the old days when cattle were forced to swim across the narrows from the island into Cowal. The crossing takes about five minutes. On the other side of the Kyles is (strangely) the continuation of the A886, which offers a straight run of 8 miles to Rothesay. Bute is a small island, about 15 miles long and 3 miles wide. Yet it has an infinite variety of scenery from the wilder northern end to the gentler landscape of the south. Rothesay is the capital which has the air of being more at home with the south of England than of a Scottish island town. It is a most popular holiday resort and is geared to satisfying virtually all the needs of the visitor.

Rothesay might seem a product of only a century ago. In fact the burgh's first Royal Charter was granted in 1401 and its obligatory castle dates from around 1098. An interesting link with the castle, and indeed Rothesay, is that in 1398, King Robert III of the Scots created his eldest son 'Duke of Rothesay'. That title still exists today and is held by Charles, Prince of Wales, who is also Duke of Rothesay. Visit the Bute Museum, across from Mansion House, a fine example of Scots domestic architecture. The museum is devoted to all aspects of the Isle of Bute.

The visitor to Rothesay might well be intrigued

Glendaruel

Colintraive

Rothesay

by the town's mild temperate climate. This is the
effect of the warm Gulf Stream which bathes all
Scotland's west coast and allows such exotic
plants as palm trees and azaleas to flourish.

If time allows, before the return to Dunoon
some hours should be spent on Bute, for it has
many attractions. Sandy beaches, easy hill-
walking, fishing and other activities can be
enjoyed. Try, too, the colourful gardens and
aviary at Ardencraig. Visit Woodend, the house
built by Edmund Kean, the great English actor
of the nineteenth century, who wrote: 'How
glorious from the loopholes of retreat, to peep on
such a world'. Try a cruise on the *Waverley*, the
last sea-going paddle steamer in the world. There
is plenty in Bute to see and do and write home
about!

Port Bannatyne, Isle of Bute

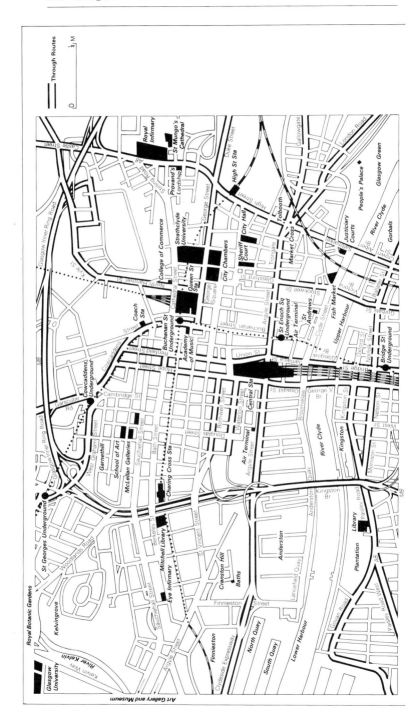

Glasgow

Tourist Information Centre
George Square, tel 221 7371/2, 221 6136/7

Population 762,288

Theatres
Theatre Royal, Hope Street
Apollo Centre, Renfield Street
Citizens' Theatre, 119 Gorbals Street
King's Theatre, Bath Street
Pavilion Theatre, Renfield Street

Cinemas
ABC 1 and 2, Sauchiehall Street
Classic, Renfield Street
Classic Grand, Jamaica Street
Coliseum, Eglinton Street
Curzon Continental, Sauchiehall Street
Glasgow Film Theatre, Rose Street
Scala, Sauchiehall Street
Odeon Film Centre, Renfield Street
Regent, Renfield Street

Places of Interest

Glasgow Cathedral. This is Glasgow's most important building,
featuring a variety of architectural styles from the thirteenth century
onwards. Though its exterior looks unpromising, with decades of
smoke-blackened stonework, the interior is something of a builders'
triumph. Carved ceiling bosses catch the eye. Clustered columns with
fine flowered capitals vie for attention with rich vaulting, numerous
monuments and regimental flags. A rare atmosphere of serenity
pervades the building, and it is a sanctuary from the city's noise and
bustle.

Provand's Lordship, Castle Street. This is Glasgow's oldest house, built
about 1471. Now a museum, it has a number of displays of seventeenth-
century furniture, tapestry and pictures.

Art Gallery and Museum, Kelvingrove Park. The museum has displays
featuring military weapons and armoury, engineering, history, natural
history and archaeology. The Central Hall is sometimes used for organ
recitals. The art gallery contains paintings, sculpture, ceramics and
jewellery. Perhaps the most impressive painting is Salvador Dali's
'Christ of St John of the Cross'. There is a collection of European
paintings in the 'Continental Wing'. There are also sculptures by
Rodin and Epstein among others.

Hunterian Museum, Gilmorehill. This is part of the Glasgow
University buildings in Kelvingrove. The University itself was founded

in 1451. The museum contains many archaeological exhibits and there is a marvellous collection of Chinese jade.

Tree Fossil Grove, Dumbarton Road. In 1887, when this park was being created, stumps of fossilised trees were discovered dating from 230 million years ago. What can be seen is not petrified wood but rather the casts formed by mud which then set within the bark of the trees. It was the trees of this type which eventually formed Scotland's massive coal deposits.

Museum of Transport, Albert Drive. This was established in 1964 and is one of the biggest collections of its kind of forms of transport ranging from horsedrawn vehicles to motor cars, bicycles, railway engines and caravans. A display of shipping is located in the Clyde Room.

People's Palace, Glasgow Green. This is a building dating from 1898 which began life as a cultural centre for the folk of Glasgow living at the eastern end of the city. It is now a museum with a comprehensive review of the story of Glasgow from 1715 to the present day. The Winter Gardens house tropical plants and birds. Part of the display is devoted to the history of the cinema and theatre in the city.

River Clyde. It is perhaps a pity that the city fathers of Glasgow did not use the River Clyde as a focal point for planning, if only to provide some pleasant vistas among the city's architecture. These omissions are now being put right and one can enjoy some pleasant walks along the restored quays which once were busy with small passenger ships taking Glasgow folk to the holiday resorts at the mouth of the river.

On the outskirts of the city are a few other attractions:

Botanic Gardens, off Great Western Road. These gardens were founded in 1841 beside the River Kelvin and contain a bewildering range of plants, from rare orchids to herbs.

Pollok House, Pollokshaws Road. This is an art gallery housing an astonishing collection of paintings, sculpture, glass, furniture, porcelain and silver. The collection of Spanish paintings is particularly fine and includes representative works by Goya, Murillo and El Greco.

Rouken Glen. Despite the feeling one has of Glasgow being a built-up city, there are many parks which serve as welcome lungs and where one can relax in surroundings away from bricks, mortar and traffic. One such is Rouken Glen, about 5 miles to the south of the city. It is one of the favourites of Glasgow folk, possibly because much of the park is still in a natural state.

Glasgow is the biggest city in Scotland, with a large population and a reputation for being an industrial sprawl. Yet those who make an effort, and not a particularly strenuous one at that, to discover what the city has to offer will be amply rewarded. Its industrial and commercial reputation rose in the eighteenth century when the city's first wave of prosperity came with the tobacco trade. The wealthy tobacco barons, as they were called, laid out much of their money on large houses and gardens, investing in property development. After tobacco came cloth. Then came ship-building on the banks of the River Clyde. It was this industry which made Glasgow world famous, for the ships that were launched from the many shipyards were household names, particularly the ocean-going liners such as the *Queen Mary*, and the two *Queen Elizabeth* ships. Many of the Royal Navy's ships were built on Clydeside, in yards which, though now under new names, still maintain the old trade of building the world's shipping.

It was inevitable that all this industrial activity would produce the development of a kind of housing which was intended to concentrate the maximum number of people in the smallest possible area: tenement buildings which eventually fell into a ruinous condition and which are only now being cleared away in an attempt to recover the former beauty of Glasgow. Even so, the first impression the visitor gets is that of a smoke-clad city which needs a sunlit day to show off its buildings in a good light. Victorian buildings are seen everywhere, some now being cleaned and restored to display their former character. New and modern buildings, not always blessed with an individual character, rise on sites where the tenements once stood in delapidated condition, their former populations dispersed to new housing areas on the outskirts of the city. But one should look twice at Glasgow's Victorian heritage, for the city was second to none in its time for its enthusiasm to translate the period of Queen Victoria into architectural stone.

Despite its industrial reputation, Glasgow is an ancient city dating from the seventh century, when its first inhabitants decided to live in the shadow of the religious cell of St Ninian, where Glasgow Cathedral now represents this ancient connection. Thereafter Glasgow grew slowly and relatively peacefully during the ensuing centuries. There were, however, a few historical incidents. In 1300, the Scots patriot, William Wallace, defeated the English at Bell o' the Brae, which site is now the upper part of High Street. In 1568, the army of Mary Queen of Scots was defeated at Langside, near Queen's Park. And in the Jacobite Rising of 1745, Glasgow saw the pride of the times, Bonnie Prince Charlie. The Prince, however, did not make himself popular with the City fathers, for he demanded the sum of £15,000 and all the arms in the city.

Getting about in Glasgow is easy, by using the excellent bus services and the underground train services. But the flavour of the city is best obtained by sightseeing on foot.

The refurbishing of Glasgow's old buildings has been mentioned already and the results are impressive to say the least. The visitor is recomended to visit a few of the places now presenting a fresh clean face to the world. Just past Glasgow Cross (end of Argyle Street) there are examples of the new art form: painting on a large scale on the gable-ends of tenement buildings. In Sauchiehall Street the former Willow Tearooms, where the Scots architect Charles Rennie Mackintosh did some marvellous design work, has been converted as a jeweller's shop, after considerable restoration. Also at Glasgow Cross one can admire the newly-opened vista of the seventeenth-century tolbooth Steeple which is all that remains of the larger building of 1626. The city's planners have also given thought to the closing of sections of some streets to traffic, creating pedestrian precincts. They can be found on Sauchiehall Street, Argyle Street and Buchanan Street and are oases of quiet with the distant noise of traffic only faintly heard. Even such functional structures as Central Station have been given a face-clean and can now be admired in their former glory. Tourists, indeed, need not think twice about visiting Glasgow. Much is rising from the smoke-grimed ashes of over a century.

Glasgow has always been a cosmopolitan city and this is reflected in the wide choice of eating places, many offering ethnic foods. One of the latter is the *Koh-I-Noor*, specialising in Punjabi foods. One restaurant which consistently figures in good-food guides is the *Ubiquitous Chip* on Byres Road (off Dumbarton Road). The Italian community in Glasgow has been established for such a long time now that one might expect some Italian eating places to be a feature of the city, and one is not disappointed. *La Laterna* (bottom end of Hope Street and handy for a visit to the *Theatre Royal*) has been recommended by the writer's grapevine, with some tantalising highlights on offer. *Caruso's* (opposite the *Theatre Royal*), *Pippino's* (on Hyndland Street) and *La Terrazza* (corner of Sauchiehall Street and Westminster Terrace) have also received favourable mentions by scouts.

As might be expected, Glasgow also provides a wide range of entertainment. It is the home of the Scottish Ballet and the Scottish National Orchestra. Theatre-goers are well catered for, with the *Citizens' Theatre* (Gorbals Street) presenting many productions by Scottish playwrights.

Index